D1195907

THE LAST CHAPTER

The facts about the last days of Grumman

JAKE BUSSOLINI

Edited by: C.H. "Skip" Weber

authorHOUSE®

AuthorHouse™
1663 Liberty Drive
Bloomington, IN 47403
www.authorhouse.com
Phone: 1-800-839-8640

© *2014 Jake Bussolini. All rights reserved.*

No part of this book may be reproduced, stored in a retrieval system, or transmitted by any means without the written permission of the author.

Published by AuthorHouse   11/06/2014

ISBN: 978-1-4969-5174-8 (sc)
ISBN: 978-1-4969-5172-4 (hc)
ISBN: 978-1-4969-5173-1 (e)

Library of Congress Control Number: 2014919878

Any people depicted in stock imagery provided by Thinkstock are models, and such images are being used for illustrative purposes only. Certain stock imagery © Thinkstock.

Because of the dynamic nature of the Internet, any web addresses or links contained in this book may have changed since publication and may no longer be valid. The views expressed in this work are solely those of the author and do not necessarily reflect the views of the publisher, and the publisher hereby disclaims any responsibility for them.

Contents

Dedication

This book is dedicated to the thousands of Grumman men and women and their families who contributed so much of themselves to the company. Grumman was a company that attributed its success to the loyalty and dedication of its employees.

Memorial

This book is dedicated to the memory of Brian C. Weber, eldest son of Skip and Betsy Weber, who passed away much too young on August 11, 2014. He fought a lifelong battle with Klippel-Trenaunay Syndrome (KTS), ultimately succumbing to it at the youthful age of 38. He will be missed by all who knew him.

"Either write something worth doing or
do something worth writing"

Benjamin Franklin

Contributors

I would like to thank the following people for their interest and contributions to the content of this book:

George Smith, for his tireless efforts to search for and find written information supporting the facts for the time frame of events of this book.

John Ballow and his associates Nice Croce, Rick Vitelli and Michael Davidowski for researching much of the financial history that helped define the critical nature of Grumman's financial status.

Andy Ballow, for his input concerning facts of Grumman's inventory reduction program.

Clyde Stover, for his assistance with the facts surrounding some political activities.

Dr.Renso Caporali, for his validation of much of his activity during the critical period surrounding the acquisition of Grumman by Northrop.

Weyman (Sandy) Jones, for supplying assistance based on his long experience as an accomplished author and his memories as a Grumman executive.

Dan Knowles, for his input and advice related to the cultural history of Grumman and its employees.

Several Former Grumman employees provided bit-and-piece inputs including: Dick Anderson, Harry Milne, and Bob Foster.

James Roche, for his continued friendship and valuable insight into the inner workings of Northrop during the critical acquisition period. He also validated many of the activities that took place during the integration of the two companies.

Kent Kresa, for his review and verification of several of the critical events that took place prior to the acquisition. I must also recognize Kent for his desire to retain the Grumman name and his efforts to follow his strategic vision to build a new and stronger company.

Introduction

It was July 2nd 1962 when I first walked through the doors of Plant 5 in Bethpage, New York as a new employee of The Grumman Aircraft Engineering Corporation. As an electrical engineer, there were few of my kind there because until now, structures, aerodynamics and other aircraft skills were the ones in demand. But now Grumman had a couple of more complex electronic aircraft the A-2F and the W-2F and the company needed more electronics experience. (The A-2F was later designated as the A-6 and the W-2F was designated as the E-2)

I was escorted to my desk on the third floor, a plain gray desk with a gray chair, exactly like the sea of hundreds of other desks that cluttered the third floor. Few walls separated the different departments and just a few small bullpens that were occupied by the Section Heads. There was an ash tray on every desk because just about everyone in the building was a smoker. No air conditioning, just tall industrial fans scattered throughout the area. Coffee was purchased from a vending machine for a dime and it was only considered appropriate to get coffee during the break periods in the morning and afternoon. Cigarettes were also purchased from vending machines for twenty five cents a pack.

I learned very quickly that the important people were the ones who worked behind the Engineering Counter. They controlled the pencils and paper and just about everything else that was needed to get your job done. No computers were in sight. A fellow named Mark Gus, the tallest guy on the floor, ran the only computer in the building. Every two desks shared a telephone and no personal calls were permitted except in an emergency. Starting time for everyone was 8:12 am and quitting time was 4:42pm. Lunch break was 30 minutes. Communications between people back then actually resulted from people talking to each other face to face. There was no e mail, no twitter, no texting. One might wonder how we actually survived in that environment!

My first direction from my Section Head was to go to the Engineering Counter and get supplies and an engineering notebook. I was familiar with that practice because my previous employer, The Hazeltine Corporation, also required that engineers document all of their work in registered notebooks. All engineers used slide rules at that time but you had to supply your own. If you had to add or subtract numbers, you actually used long hand supported by, of all things, your own brain.

I can't remember exactly what went through my mind at the end of my first day of work. I do know that I would never have dreamed that thirty two years later, I would have worked my way up through the organization to become a Senior Vice president of the company, just handed an assignment the results of which would change the nature of Grumman forever.

For thousands of Grumman employees, the Apollo Program was the highlight of our career. We all took great pride and personal satisfaction that our company designed and built the Lunar Module that delivered Astronauts to the moon and brought them safely back to Earth.

The Apollo Lunar Module, also known as the Lunar Excursion Module was designed and built by Grumman. This was the lunar landing portion of the Apollo spacecraft that brought astronauts to the moon six times between 1969 and 1972. The Lunar Module never suffered any failures that impacted a lunar mission. Apollo 13's Lunar Module exceeded its performance requirements by maintaining life support for astronauts after an explosion damaged the Apollo Service Module.(NASA supplied photo.)

Now, however, the glory days were over. The Government was making significant cuts in defense spending and Grumman was becoming a victim of those cuts. As the Corporate Senior Vice President of Strategy and Technology, it was my job to help put together the strategies that would guide the company into the future. But now the future seemed dim, we were facing serious reductions in our work force that would take place as soon as the F-14 program came to a halt in two years. The F-14 program kept thousands of people employed throughout its production life. Just about every member of Grumman's management participated in the fight to keep the F-14 alive. Without the F-14 and with the A-6 program nearing completion, it would probably be impossible to maintain Grumman's position as a prime contractor for military aircraft.

The News Arrives

August 16, 1992 was a typical day in Bethpage. At the Grumman Headquarters facility it was business as usual trying to keep up with events in Washington, reviewing current program status, preparing briefings to answer customer requests, and the other business of keeping a Fortune 100 company functioning. My phone rang at about 2 pm and I was told to be at Chairman Renso Caporali's office at 2:30. My office was only a short distance from his office on the third floor and as I walked toward his office for the meeting I saw that Caporali's door was closed, the first signal that this might not be a routine meeting. Caporali took his responsibilities as CEO of Grumman very seriously, but his personality was such that his door was rarely closed. One hallmark of the Grumman culture was its open door policy, the idea that the door of every member of management was always open to the employees. This didn't necessarily refer to actual physically open doors at all times, but out of tradition, executive doors were usually left open, except when confidential business was being conducted.

As I approached the office, other invited executives were also approaching. These included Bob Myers, company President, Bob Anderson, CFO, and the company's three senior Vice Presidents; Tom Kane, Steve Daly, and me.

From the expression on each of our faces, we all seemed to know instinctively that this was not an ordinary meeting. Caporali held regularly scheduled staff meetings that we all attended, so why this special get together? The door opened and we were invited into the office. Caporali was a serious fellow but he always had a jovial greeting for you when you entered his office. This was his technique to break any tension that might have existed because you were meeting with the top guy. But today it was different. There was no deflective greeting: we were just told to sit at the conference table. The office door closed and sensing the tension, we all sat in silence. Caporali was standing behind his desk facing the windows that overlooked the Grumman campus. It was like he was waiting, trying to find the right sound or the right movement to break the silence.

As he turned and walked toward the table, he started his dialog slowly and softly. His first few words seemed to be caught in his throat, like they just didn't want to come out. There was a slight trembling, but the words were still very clear. "Gentlemen, I just received a call from a very reliable source in the Navy and the message was not good. We have exercised every avenue available to us and the Navy has done the same, but we must now accept the fact that there are no more extensions to the F-14 program and a similar fate applies to the A-6 program. This is a day that we all feared deep inside us, would come someday, but we hoped we could prolong it a little longer. The Navy has decided to go with the upgraded F-18 and there is no longer any possibility that we can turn that around. We thought we had effectively made our case that the money to upgrade the F-14 has already been spent and the upgraded system is already flying. The F-18 upgrade on the other hand is yet to be started. We thought our story made the greatest sense, but in these times of political override, anything can happen and it did. The power brokers in Washington chose the more expensive route. The F-14 program is over."

Having finally managed to get these unpleasant words out, Caporali pulled his chair around to the conference table and we sat as a group as he went on, as though trying to lighten the tone.

"Now for the bad news. As we look ahead, without those two programs, there is no way that Grumman can continue as a prime defense weapon system contractor. Our revenue stream will carry us a year or two, but we must take steps right now to plot a new direction for the company and do it in a serious and expeditious manner. Over the last three years we have all worked tirelessly to emphasize shareholder value for this company. The results have been very rewarding. We have come a long way toward eliminating our debt. We have improved the efficiency of our operations and raised our share price from its low of $13 to its current value of $24. This puts us in a fairly good position for some sort of partnering, but we are not yet financially strong enough to make any meaningful acquisitions that would allow us remain a strong prime contractor contender."

A suggestion was made that we consider filing a complaint against the Navy, alleging that the F -18 upgrade would result in a completely new and different aircraft. That being the case, the effort should be put out for competitive bid. Caporali felt that a complaint against our largest customer was probably not the wisest thing to do.

It took all of us a minute to grasp the meaning of Caporali's words, but each of us, in our own way, knew that this was the end of Grumman as we had grown to know and love it. After some idle conversation, Cappy continued his dialog. "I am asking Jake Bussolini to chair a detailed study of all our options including possible acquisitions, partnering, strategic alliances and mergers. The objective of these studies is to determine those steps necessary to permit us to continue in some manner as a prime contractor, to protect the welfare of our employees and to leverage some of our unique technology capabilities. There is a degree of urgency to these studies, but more important, they should be conducted in the strictness of confidence. We are in a period of some unusual corporate takeovers that started as innocent studies. I don't want word of this work to leak out and turn this into a hostile takeover that we will all regret."

Caporali further charged that this executive team would be briefed periodically on the progress of the studies and when necessary he would brief the Board Of Directors. Of course, everyone's total cooperation was expected during the course of the studies.

This was not the Renso Caporali that I had known for more than 30 years. This was a CEO who had taken all of the hard actions necessary to bring Grumman back from the brink of financial disaster. During his first two years in office he had made those hard decisions which didn't always put him in favor with all of his critics. But he had succeeded in those efforts only to now see our most important programs disappear, probably changing the image, the culture and the face of Grumman forever.

Grumman had tried several ventures into non-traditional businesses in the past, but most of those ventures had left the company in serious financial trouble. By the early 1990's management had taken the necessary steps to strengthen the company's financial position, but it was still not strong enough financially to make the necessary acquisitions to grow our core capabilities. Attempts were made to build the company's electronics and data systems capability by acquisitions but our efforts to outbid the competitors, who had much stronger financing ability, were not successful.

The only alternative left was to attempt to align ourselves with another company through a friendly combination or merger. We spent nearly a year attempting to complete a friendly merger with The Northrop Corporation. This type of merger might have lessened the trauma, but change was inevitable. The merger effort eventually turned into a hostile acquisition of Grumman by Northrop.

The acquisition took place 20 years ago. There are few people still alive who know exactly how events changed and why they changed as they did. There are only often misleading news reports and rumors that have described the events that led up to the acquisition of Grumman by Northrop. As part of the very small group of Grumman executives who participated in all of the activities of that last year, I am compelled to tell the true story as it really happened. There will be no attempt in this book to shade the facts and no attempt to purposely make anyone look good or bad. To properly tell the story, I cannot simply start with the events of the 1990's. Events that took place long before paved the way toward creating the company as it existed in the 1990's. Those events and personalities need to be described for a complete understanding of how Grumman came to be what it was and what it is today.

Grumman had a proud history and was an integral part of many of the important events that shaped our great country. It is important that the documentation of Grumman's history be completed by telling the facts of the inside events that led to its final days. Having been selected by Northrop to help lead the integration of the two companies, I was permitted a unique inside look at our new owners, their personalities and their culture.

A book describing the early history of Grumman was "**The Grumman Story**" written by Richard Thruelsen and published in 1976. This book described the proud history of the company from its start on January 2, 1930 in a garage in Baldwin, New York.

A second book titled "**Inside The Iron Works**" was written by George Skurla and William Gregory and was published in 2004. That book told of many of the personalities within Grumman and covered much of the same time frame as the earlier book. Although published in 2004, the authors were not privileged to many of the events that took place leading to what has become Northrop Grumman.

I have been asked why I waited 20 years to document this unpublished history. I simply felt in justice to this great company, the **last chapter** had to be written and the facts laid straight. The facts are true to the best of my memory. I may have a date or two slightly off and if I am speculating on some event, I will clearly state that speculation. There are a couple of events that I cannot explain but I assure the readers that everything in this book is true to the best of my ability to document **the last chapter** in the history of Grumman.

Chapter One

The Defense Marketplace and Geo-Politics

Most people outside the defense industry and many that work inside it have little understanding of the complexities of doing business inside this sector. For most of the years that we remember prior to and including the President Reagan years, the defense industry was living "high off the hog." During many of those years the United States was either engaged in a skirmish or conflict (because we didn't declare war), or we were engaged in the cold war with the Soviet Union. Defense spending during that period was pretty much based on what the military commanders needed to achieve their tactical and strategic objectives. The government was discharging its constitutional obligation and approving a federal budget each fiscal year. There were few if any arguments about the extent of defense spending, but there was an increasing amount of political input into the budget process.

The contract award process during those cold war years was fairly straight forward. The Armed Services or NASA would solicit proposals from qualified companies. Each interested company would prepare preliminary designs and concepts hopefully satisfying the customer specifications.

Each proposal was priced including proposed contract terms. Supposedly, if the designs of the bidding companies satisfied the customer specifications, the company with the lowest price or the most creative solution was awarded the contract. During the 1960's and 70's there was a great deal of technological development in aerospace design and manufacturing. New technologies were finding their way into military products, often increasing the risk of failure for both the contractors and the procuring agencies. The government agencies and military services recognized this risk and their procurement policies were adjusted to accommodate it. This was the era of the "cost plus" contract, where companies were paid for all of the cost expended, plus they were paid a fee as profit. This financing technique was a "no risk" situation for contractors but it presented serious budgetary challenges for the government. It wasn't ever possible to know exactly how much a given procurement would cost. Nearly every government program exceeded its original monetary target. When this happened, the traditional congressional investigations would take place and everyone would start pointing fingers at the other side. Inevitably the contractor would be blamed for all cost increases.

During this same era, the changing technology demands were causing enormous capital investments by companies desiring to do business in the government contracting arena.

Existing procurement procedures permitted these companies to amortize their capital investments over a specified number of expected production products, which allowed these companies to eventually recover these investments over a long period of time. This became a financial trap for contractors.

In order for a particular service agency to justify the cost of new programs, the program projections for the number of items to be procured were greatly exaggerated. These were the quantities that companies used to calculate the return on their capital investments. When the procurement quantities were eventually reduced in subsequent fiscal years, prices had to be raised to compensate for the reduced numbers. This procurement merry-go round just kept turning and each year the fiscal screws were tightened more and more on the companies that were "lucky enough" to have won the original contract.

This problem was further complicated with the advent of fixed price contracting. Despite continuing annual budget squeezes, contractors were now required to offer fixed prices for their products, using some form of crystal ball to project possible future procurement quantities. Now, all of the risk was placed on the shoulders of the defense industry, but strict procurement rules still placed severe restrictions on profit levels.

This is where politics began to play a more significant role in the defense procurement process. Congress was the mechanism by which fiscal budgets were reviewed and approved. When the procurement numbers changed from one year to another causing cost increases, pressure got more intense for Congress to begin holding the line on costs. Program budget reductions meant layoffs among government contractors and now it became a process of protecting the economic interests of congressional constituents. No Congressman wanted to face his or her constituents and justify why they permitted budget reductions causing layoffs in their district. Individual political power took on a new meaning because those politicians, congressmen and senators, who had gained seniority within their individual committees, were the ones who wielded the real power in the budget reviews, especially committee and subcommittee chair persons. These powerful committee leaders had the power to "mark" a budget line item, and once marked, that item was rarely challenged. If your company happened to be located in a district represented by one of these powerful congressmen, your programs were likely to receive a more favorable action during the budget review process. You won't find this process described like this anywhere else, but believe me, this is the way the system really worked.

This is where John O'Brien (at the time Grumman's president) felt that Grumman was at a distinct disadvantage in the government contracting arena. The only local Long Island congressman that ever had any real power base to help Grumman with its budget battles was Congressman Joe Addabbo. Addabbo was a democrat and not exactly a strong supporter of defense spending. He did however hold a significant position in Congress as Chairman of the House Appropriations Subcommittee on Defense. Although Addabbo was an outspoken opponent of President Reagan' defense spending increases, he did make himself available to Grumman to hear about our budgetary problems and sometimes acted in our behalf. Other than Congressman Addabbo, Long Island voters had a tendency to want to throw out their congressional representatives every few years so that none were ever able to gain the seniority required for a position of strong committee power. Congressman Addabbo died in April of 1985 ending any political edge that Grumman had.

Congressman Tom Downey represented New York's 2nd District on Long Island from 1975 until 1993. Congressman Downey was on the Ways and Means Committee and served as acting chairman of that committee for five years. He was also on the Armed Service Committee, but had little seniority there. Congressman Downey was always interested in Grumman's budgetary problems and often opened some doors to people that might help us. He could do nothing directly to directly help Grumman, again because he had no real position of influence.

In September of 1988 John O'Brien gave a speech to the leaders of Long Island Industry at a meeting of the Long Island Association that sent shock waves through the areas business and political circles. O'Brien was the type of person that did not believe in being subtle. He was usually outspoken and rarely held back his thoughts. He warned that without a regional effort to solve many of the problems of the area, like clogged highways, lack of affordable housing, and high electricity costs, the economic growth of the Long Island region would stall. He predicted that the days of continuing heavy industry on Long Island were over.

O'Brien warned that the cost of doing business on Long Island were so high that it would be nearly impossible to attract any new manufacturing to the area. In reviewing Grumman's activities in recent years, O'Brien indicated that by the end of that year (1988) Grumman would have reduced its work force of 23,500 by about another 2,300 jobs. Research and development spending had already been cut from 46.3 million dollars in 1987 to less than 30 million dollars in 1988. Grumman had also reduced its capital spending from 175 million dollars in 1987 to 150 million in 1988. Although most of the Long Island business leaders who heard the speech were shocked by the bluntness of his delivery, none really disagreed with its content.

At this public meeting, O'Brien treaded lightly on Long Island's weak political position, but in the confines of his office, our political weakness drove his passion for change. O'Brien was not willing to sit back and let these disturbing trends take an additional toll on the company. He ordered me to do a comprehensive study of the geo-political makeup of the Defense industry, specifically those companies with whom Grumman competed. He felt that Grumman was at a distinct disadvantage because of its New York location both economically and politically. He believed deeply that Grumman's future was dim if we did not move at least 50% of our operations to areas that offered better economic and political benefits than New York.

At the same time O'Brien directed Tom Kane, Vice President of Marketing, to work with the Washington office to set up monthly breakfast meetings with invitations to all of New York's congressional representatives. O'Brien would personally attend each of these meetings in Washington to brief our congressional representatives on activities within Grumman and programs that were of importance to the company. O'Brien indicated that he wanted every one of our representatives to be completely briefed on all of our areas of interest and potential funding problems that might need their attention. With full awareness of Grumman's budget problems, our representatives would at least be prepared to make the appropriate arguments in our favor.

The Washington office scheduled these breakfast meetings at strategic times that they knew congressional representatives would be available. The first scheduled meeting got fairly good attendance from the Congressmen and their staff. The second meeting started to see a fall off in attendance with most of the attendees being congressional staff members. I attended the fourth breakfast meeting with the intent to present our finding on our geo-political studies. The only attendees at that meeting were Grumman employees. Not one congressman or member of their staff attended. On the plane back to New York, O'Brien turned to those of us seated near him and said, "That's what is wrong with doing business in New York."

In contrast to that occasion, let me introduce a short true story here. As part of O'Brien's plan to move portions of Grumman outside the New York area, consideration was being given to moving the headquarters of Grumman's Space Division to Texas, closer to the NASA Johnson Space Center. We had been investigating that possibility along with a couple of other locations for some time. Meanwhile Tom Kane and the Washington office had been working their way through some congressional committee reviews of our A-6 funding.

Things were not looking good but progress was being made slowly.

The Grumman A-6 Intruder was a twin jet, mid-wing all weather attack aircraft. The Intruder was designed as a precision strike attack aircraft that carried the Navy and Marine Corps ground-attack/strike mission from 1963 through 1997.(Photo Supplied by the Navy)

I was working late one evening and I got a call from the Grumman Operator telling me that Congressman Jim Wright's office was on the phone and wanted to be briefed the next morning on our budgetary problem. I took the call and promised to have someone in Washington the next morning. After briefing John O'Brien I was told to do the briefing myself. It was too late to make other arrangements. I was familiar with the A-6 funding problem so I gathered some material and called Congressman Wright's office to finalize the meeting time. This was to be no normal meeting for me. Congressman Jim Wright was not only a Texas Congressman, he was the Speaker of the House of Representatives, the third most powerful politician in Washington. I was told to call the office of Congressman Jack Brooks to arrange to meet him first thing in the morning. Congressman Brooks, also from Texas, would be my host. He would lead me to the Speakers office for our meeting.

I didn't do much sleeping that night. I needed to do some catch-up research on Texas politics. I wasn't about to brief just another congressman. Congressman Jim Wright had been elected to Congress in 1955 and was made Speaker of the House in 1975. This was the man that was third in line to be President. It was 1988 and the presidential election fever had taken over Washington. Jack Brooks was a long term Congressman from Beaumont, Texas. When I arrived in Washington the next morning, I went directly to the office of Congressman Brooks. His secretary was thoroughly briefed on my arrival and took me right into Congressman Brooks' office. Meeting this man in itself was quite an experience. He was a big man with a gruff voice and hands that looked like a lumberjack's hands. He was loud and used as many four letter words as he could remember. He asked me for a real quick briefing on our A-6 budget problem and off we went to meet the Speaker. I'm positive that he didn't hear a word that I said when I briefed him.

When we arrived at the Speakers office, his secretary informed us that the Speaker was on the floor of Congress but he had instructed her to notify him when I arrived and he would leave the floor for his office. We sat for about 30 minutes as I watched several men and women enter his office. None of them had left and Congressman Brooks knew every one of them. Then I was beckoned into the office. I can't even remember how nervous I must have been.

Speaker Wright was a small man and very pleasant. He was sitting at his desk in this massive office with about a dozen others seated in rows opposite his desk. I was asked to sit in the chair aside his desk. The Speaker started the conversation by apologizing to me that those that were seated there were only a few of the Texas delegation that he was able to round up at the last minute. There were a total of 12 congressman seated there. As he introduced them to me including their party affiliation he looked at me directly and said, "please note that these people are both Democrats and Republicans and their party affiliation means nothing in this room, we are all Texans and that is what's important."

The Speaker introduced me as a Vice President of The Grumman Corporation, a company that is considering locating its Space Division in Texas. He also said that he understood that we had a small funding problem that needed attention and that I had ten minutes to make the case. I made a brief presentation of the budget problem and he offered some back and forth discussion which took nearly fifteen minutes. He pointed to one or two congressmen and gave them actions, asking them to report back to Congressman Brooks. He directed Congressman Brooks to take me to meet Senator Lloyd Bentsen, just to have me meet him. Congressman Wright shook my hand and indicated that things would be handled and he left the office.

Congressman Brooks led me out of the office after personally introducing me to everyone that was in attendance. We went over to the Senate Office Building to meet Senator Bentsen. When we arrived at Senator Bentsen's office it was total chaos. It had just been announced that Senator Bentsen had been picked by Michael Dukakis to be his Vice Presidential running mate. Needless to say, no meeting took place that day. When I said goodbye to Congressman Brooks, he shook my hand and asked that I keep him informed about our possible move of the Space Division to Texas. That was their motivation to help us.

I include this story as an indication of how well tuned and well organized the Texas political organization is. The movement of Grumman's Space Division to Texas could not be considered a monumental event. It was however important enough that the a large number of the Texas Congressional delegation including the Speaker of the House showed enough interest to help us make that decision.

Some weeks after my meeting with the Speaker in Washington, I was asked to speak at a meeting of a local Long Island Accountants group. During that speech I gave a brief summary of Grumman's programs and opened the meeting for questions. I was asked to explain why Grumman felt that Long Island didn't offer the same political advantage that other areas did. In my response to that question, I told about the breakfast meetings in Washington and the apparent lack of interest by the Long Island delegation. In contrast I summarized my experience with the Texas politicians and how they responded to our problem. Apparently one of Congressman Downey's staff was in attendance at that meeting and the next day I received a call from the Congressman's office asking why I had made the comment. I replied to the Congressman's staffer by asking if he knew about the breakfast meetings and he indicated that he did know. I then asked him if the Congressman had attended and he indicated that he had not, nor had his staff. My response was "I rest my case."

John O'Brien had been blunt with his comments to the Long Island business leaders, but he knew that by himself he could do little to fix those problems. What he could do, however, was prepare a plan to move half of the company's future programs off Long Island to a more favorable political climate, hence his order to me to do a geo/political study so we could make more informed decisions about future locations. O'Brien knew that his feelings about the New York political situation were correct, but he wanted an independent analytical confirmation of that, including some recommended solutions.

At about the same time O'Brien had ordered the geo-political study, I had received the resume of a gentleman who had worked for IBM doing some international facilities work. His name was Claude Hooton. Hooton's facilities background was of no interest to me but there were other things in his history that were interesting. He had been active in Texas politics for several years and at one point had run for office as a Congressman. He was not successful in that attempt but he had some other interesting connections that I wanted to investigate. Hooton listed his mailing address at that time as part of the Kennedy complex on Cape Cod. I found that interesting and intriguing and decided to travel to Hyannis Port, Mass. to interview Hooton.

Hooton picked me up at the Hyannis airport and during the drive to his temporary residence, he briefed me on his background. Hooton was the room mate of Ted Kennedy at

Harvard and they had remained very good friends for many years since that time. When Hooton returned from London where he had a temporary residence while working with IBM, Kennedy, at that time Senator Kennedy, offered to let him live in the guest house at Hyannis Port. While living there Hooton was doing several maintenance chores around the complex.

We arrived at the Hyannis complex around noon and Hooton proceeded to take me to the main living room of the Kennedy house. The cook made us a light lunch as we talked about Hooton's work history. As we sat in the soft chair near the room's center coffee table, I noticed a strange piece of artifact on the table. It looked like a piece of something that had been blown up. Hooton explained that this was a fragment from the embassy in London that was bombed when Joe Kennedy was the Ambassador there. At one point the matriarch of the Kennedy family, Rose Kennedy was wheeled into the room by her nurse to sit by the window. At this point I suggested that it might be better if we talked in a more private place, not wanting to disturb Mrs. Kennedy.

I found Hooton's political awareness to be exceptional. He seemed to know his way around the political system, he was outgoing and friendly and very personable. I asked Hooton if he was interested in coming on as a consultant for a few months to do a geo-political study for us. We eventually settled on an arrangement and he became a temporary consultant.

The concern that O'Brien had expressed to me was that Grumman's main location in New York was a handicap to the company because we didn't have any politicians in our region that cared in the least about the defense business. He felt that several of our main competitors had located portions of their company in areas that had very strong political power in the defense appropriations process. That power gave those companies some favorable advantage when their programs were being challenged or their budgets were being modified or eliminated.

It took Hooton about a year to come to any conclusions with his work, but the conclusions were eye-opening. The first segment of the study examined the defense spending that went to every State in the country over a ten year period. He then looked at every member of Congress including the House and Senate to see which representatives held committee positions on the key defense committees and subcommittees and who held the chairmanships of those committees. The study also looked at key Defense Department leaders and their state of residence. Also included were the Cabinet members and key executive staff.

The study also made an attempt to rank each position in terms of its power rating and the influence of that position on the decision process for defense contracts and their respective budgets. Each member of the political power base got a numerical rating depending on the influence of that position. Using these power ratings, each state was given a score based on the power base of its resident politicians and other office holders. It really was no surprise that the states with the highest power ratings had the highest levels of defense or other government program spending over the ten year period that was studied. This is exactly what John O'Brien had suspected. The results didn't imply there was any wrong doing involved, only that there was a justified concern that Grumman was not in a favorable position because of its New York location and the State's political make- up.

Based on the study results there were two things that we felt could be done, one was a short term action, the other a more strategic solution. The near term action that Grumman could take was to examine each new proposal that we were submitting, looking at how we picked our partners, the locations of our suppliers and subcontractors and score each proposal in terms of political strength. If the scores were low, we could ask the program managers to determine if there were any reasonable alternatives that would satisfy their technical and manufacturing requirements that would result in a higher score. This would only be an informal rating. Each program manager was of course required to put together the best possible technical team to satisfy program requirements.

The strategic action was to examine O'Brien's relocation plan that would place at least 50% of the company's operations outside of New York. He felt that we should direct all new work to go out of state if it was practical and cost effective to do so. We could use the rankings of the Hooton study to give some guidance for future locations

One of the more interesting facts that came from the Hooton study was the importance of the Chairman of both the House and Senate Defense Appropriations Committees and their associated sub committees. That pointed an immediate arrow toward West Virginia where Senator Robert Byrd was apparently their Senator-For- Life. West Virginia is a small state, but Byrd was known as the "pork" senator. He wielded a lot of power and was not afraid to use it for the good of his state.

O'Brien dispatched me to visit Senator Byrd and brief him on our F-14 and A-6 budgetary problems. We looked at every penny that Grumman placed in West Virginia via our sub contractors and parts suppliers. The numbers of course were not encouraging. West Virginia had a population of less than 2 million and the state was not populated with many suppliers that suited our needs but armed with the numbers such as they were, I headed for Senator Byrd's office.

When I arrived at the appointed time, I was led right to his office. As a Senior Senator his quarters were representative of his position. The office was large but not unreasonable. I didn't know what to expect of the Senator. I had done my homework on his background and personality, but you never knew what to expect on the first visit.

The Senator was gracious, asked me to sit across from him at his desk. I thought it was unusual that there was no staff member present, but apparently that was his practice. The Senator asked me my name a couple of times, and repeated it to himself several times as if this was his way of remembering. I told him of our budgetary problems with the two programs and I was satisfied that I had made the case. His reaction was very strange. He always had his chin resting on his hand, elbow propped on his desk. His eyes were always in a state of being almost closed, perhaps in a slight sleep. But I realized when he spoke he had heard every word I had said. He recited a short verse of poetry that I supposed had some connection to my visit. He then turned to me and asked why in the world he should be concerned about Grumman? He understood the numbers that I had quoted but we had no physical presence in West Virginia so why should he go out of his way to help us?

He then went into a completely different dialog."Jake," he said, "I just came from a hearing where I got $60 million appropriated for an extension to the Clarskburg West Virginia airport. Why Clarksburg you might ask. Well, it's not generally known yet but the FBI is going to re-locate their finger printing center from Washington, D.C. to Clarksburg and we need a longer runway to bring commercial airline traffic into that airport. Construction is going to start immediately. At some point in the future when I fly into the Clarksburg airport it would certainly be nice if there was a building along side the runway that had a Grumman sign on it." He went on further, "United Technology has a large facility there, Lockheed has a nice plant close to town, and a Grumman plant at the Clarksburg airport would make me feel a lot better about helping Grumman with its funding problem." We parted with the Senator handing me the business card of Congressman Alan Mollohan, one of the two West Virginia Congressmen at that time. He indicated that he would ask Congressman Mollohan to work closely with me if we needed any help with our new building.

When I returned to my office at Grumman the next morning, I had already received a message from Congressman Mollohan asking me to call him. Two weeks later Congressman Mollohan had arranged for a Grumman group to meet with local businessmen to discuss location possibilities at the

Clarksburg Airport. In the interim, we had discussions with representatives from United Technologies and Lockheed to determine the availability of a manufacturing talent base. We were assured that the talent was available and anxious to work.

After a series of internal meetings, John O'Brien decided to establish a manufacturing facility at the Clarksburg Airport to do sheet metal manufacturing of our support equipment racks and benches. Of course we made Senator Byrd aware of our decision through Congressman Mollohan.

Within days of making our decision known, I received a call from Gaston Caperton, the Governor of West Virginia to inform us that his office was available to help in any way possible to expedite completion of our new facility. When construction of the facility got underway, Governor Caperton flew to Bethpage for a social visit with Grumman people. He toured some of our facilities and he and his pilot had the opportunity to fly the Grumman simulator. Before our plant was completed, Governor Caperton was re-elected and several of us were invited to his inauguration in Charleston, West Virginia.

This was the way a small, but politically strong, state continued to demonstrate its appreciation of the Grumman presence. It may have been small, but it was powerful.

When Ronald Reagan became president in 1981, he had the challenge of following perhaps the least creative president in the country's history. Reagan was ambitious enough to undertake massive changes in the way government did business. As a strong advocate of a dominant military to build a power base that would be respected throughout the world, the Reagan era was also one where previously unheard of amounts of money would pass from Washington to the military-industrial complex to build this force. This glut of money builds prosperity, but it also breeds corruption at some point. When government money flows so fast and free, it is usually accompanied by less oversight and monitoring.

Most of today's generation is not aware of the government crackdown on military spending fraud known in the 1980's as "Operation Ill Wind". Those of us who worked in the military procurement process during those times clearly remember how the system worked and how this period will go down as one of the most corrupt periods in this country's history. It was also a time when the reputations of many large and well respected defense companies were tainted by their participation in corrupt government procurement procedures.

Because of the grandiose nature of the fraud and corruption that took place in the 1980's, there is also much history that was incorrectly written at that time. I will try to correct a small portion of that incorrect history related to Grumman.

Many of the reports of corrupt activities listed Grumman as one of the participating companies. Grumman as a company was never involved in the Ill Wind investigations. We were never named in any of the illegal transactions, never paid any bribes or received any special treatment by government officials in return for payments to them. In the course of the investigations, John O'Brien, CEO of Grumman at the time, was indirectly named through his private dealings with an individual who may have been involved. Because of Grumman's policies on such matters, O'Brien was asked to resign from his position and he honored that request. As a result of the timing of those events, Grumman is often mentioned along with other companies that were involved, but Grumman was never found guilty of any improprieties.

The Ill Wind investigations did, however, find very high level defense officials guilty of taking bribes and making decisions favorable to those who offered them money. These officials were within the top structure of the Navy and many of us were required to deal with them in the normal course of doing business. The highest level government official found guilty was one we dealt with regularly. That was Melvin Paisley, who was serving as the Assistant Secretary of The Navy under John Lehman, who was at that time Secretary of the Navy.

Paisley was formerly employed by Boeing as a Sales Manager. During that time he became acquainted with

John Lehman who was then a Consultant to Boeing. Paisley was an intelligent individual, and although often tough to deal with, had a reputation for getting the job done. When John Lehman was appointed Secretary of The Navy, he brought Paisley on board as Assistant Secretary in charge of Research and Engineering. In this position Paisley was a power house behind essentially every Navy program that was in development, and controlled billions of dollars of Navy funding. Paisley was the decision maker to get a program funded or keep program funds coming. Paisley's position required many interfaces with Grumman management.

Tom Kane and I met several times with Paisley to discuss the status of some Grumman programs. I found him to be very difficult to deal with. He was a dominant force, gave you very little time to make a case and often gave the impression that he wasn't even listening. Perhaps in retrospect, that was because we were not offering anything beyond normal program data. Paisley always had staff members present in our meetings and he would often deal harshly with his staff in our presence. Why bring up this unpleasant period in our country's history? I offer it as a reminder of how secrets were sold to competitors, how government officials were being bribed, how bids were being rigged, payoffs hidden, and favors delivered. This was the environment in which Grumman had to work and succeed. These were the people that were making the decisions that would chart our success in history.

The Ill Wind operations led to the conviction of nine government officials, forty two Washington consultants, and seven companies. The best known of the companies was United Technologies, the seventh largest defense company, Unisys, the fifteenth largest, Loral Corp., the 16th largest and Teledyne which was number thirty seven. Unisys was forced to pay fines totaling more than $150 million. Paisley was convicted and sentenced to a four year prison term.

I am not trying to portray sour grapes in our government dealings or imply that the events that I described above had any effect on the Navy's decision to abandon the F-14. What I am attempting to get across is the fact that dealing with Washington as a supplier is far more complicated than simply having the best product, or the greatest bang for the buck. The defense products business requires that a company cross many different lines, including both the user service (the Navy or Air Force) and the all-encompassing political world.

John O'Brien, during his term as the leader of the company, tried very hard to deal with the politics of this business. O'Brien wasn't the first Grumman leader to take up that challenge. Most of the Grumman leaders as far back as the founders, understood the importance of good relationships with our Washington customers. Perhaps during the early days, politics didn't play as significant a role as it now does. The first Grumman executive leader that openly understood the politics of the defense business was Lew Evans back in the late 60's. When laws were passed permitting the establishment of Political Action Committees, Evans created the Grumman version of such a committee. He called it The Long Island Citizenship Club. I am familiar with that organization because Evans asked me to be an officer in the organization. Jack Rettaliata and Tom Rozzi were the lead executives of the club. This was more of a social club that Evens could use to inform its members of goings-on in Washington. Evans concept was that Grumman needed no enemies in Washington. Any funds raised through member contributions were small in size. If requested by an individual politician for a political contribution, the organization always encouraged its member contributors to give the same amount to the opponent. The concept was to make sure Grumman didn't make anyone mad at us. The things that most members remember about this organization were the monthly social gatherings at The Holiday Manor in Bethpage. Evans would take the stage and bring everyone up to date on what was going on in Washington.

Lew Evans himself was a dynamic force on the Washington scene, probably logging as many hours traveling back and forth to Washington as any other Grumman employee. Evans knowledge of how Washington worked was largely responsible for Grumman's teaming with General Dynamics to build the tri-service F-111. Everyone knew that the armed services would never truly accept a common airplane, but that was the political money saver of the era and Lew Evans knew that eventually the Navy would want its own aircraft, which eventually became the F-14.

The F-14 tomcat is a supersonic twin engine variable sweep wing, two place strike fighter designed and built by Grumman. The multiple tasks of navigation, target acquisition, electronic counter measures and weapons deployment are divided between the pilot and the radar intercept officer. Its primary missions include precision strike against ground targets, air superiority, and fleet defense. (U.S. Navy photograph)

Chapter Two

Needing a Financial Recovery

When Lew Evans died in 1972, the active political leadership of Grumman came to an end. Certainly the company leadership that followed Evans understood the importance of political astuteness, but it wasn't until John O'Brien was appointed President of Grumman in 1986 that Grumman actively responded to the political reality. I believe O'Brien felt incredibly passionate about the price Grumman was paying for its lack of any regional political support.

I worked for O'Brien for all of the years that he was the company leader, either as President or later as CEO. I am witness to the fact that despite the tough leadership traits that O'Brien exhibited and the methods he used to get the job done, he always had the best interests of Grumman in his mind first and foremost.

The problems that O'Brien faced during his period of leadership were perhaps too much for one person to handle. To any of us close to him It was never obvious why he chose to hold both of the top positions himself, without appointing a Chief Operating Officer to handle the day-to-day operational issues. Perhaps he felt that diluting his individual power would lessen his ability to accomplish the tasks that he saw ahead of him. He clearly understood that he would never have the opportunity to move the company forward toward growth until the financial trends were reversed.

The first years of his Presidency required a great deal of his time trying to direct the continuing campaign to keep the F-14 alive. Perhaps his effort on behalf of the F-14 program dragged him too deeply into the political quagmire that was eventually his downfall. His effort to broaden Grumman's political support nationally might have become a double edged sword. He did make a great deal of progress in that arena doing so, but it is also rumored that he may have made some dangerous political enemies.

The John O'Brien period of leadership at Grumman must be broken into two segments. The first segment was the period between 1986 and 1988 when Jack Bierwirth was CEO and O'Brien was President. The second period was between 1988 and 1990, the period when O'Brien wore two hats as both Corporate President and CEO.

During his term as Corporate President, he recognized that much of his long range strategy for the company would be impossible to achieve until the company's financial position was improved. Corporate debt was rising, but as President there was little that he could do directly except to try to maximize revenue from the on-going programs. The overall finances of the company were in the hands of the CEO and his CFO. Of course, as Chief Operating Officer he could make internal operating changes that would bring overhead costs down and he did get programs going to accomplish that goal.

His first major efficiency improvement program was to bring in the McKinsey Group, an organization that was known for its ability to lead a company's internal cost reduction programs. O'Brien assigned Steve Daly and me as co-leaders of this cost reduction effort.

The goal of the first stage of this program was to take a minimum of $100 million out of the company's costs. The company was carrying two types of inventory. Contractual material was purchased for ongoing programs and was generally covered by program progress payments which were between 80% and 90% of acquisition cost. Contractual materials were normally purchased to a strict bill of materials that reflected the "as built" configuration so there was little excess. Indirect material, however, was purchased based upon past usage and these inventories amounted to more than $100 million. One of the first areas attacked by the McKinsey group was a company- wide inventory reduction program. The goal was to reduce or eliminate the maximum amount of indirect inventory.

A massive program called the Integrated Supplier Program was established as a cooperative effort between the Material Management and Procurement departments. This program called for finding one supplier that would manage an entire commodity including a total or partial buy-back of all existing inventory. When implemented, these new "just in time" inventory programs saved more than $50 million in costs, including both material costs, reductions in warehouse space and the associated labor involved in managing all of the commodities. Many of the benefits of this program were not realized until the mid 1990's.

The McKinsey cost reduction efforts also placed emphasis on reducing overhead costs in all other areas and each operating unit was required to implement indirect cost reduction efforts, most of which resulted in fewer operating personnel doing indirect tasks.

The reason that the cost reduction effort was concentrated on reducing indirect cost, was the continuing argument with the Navy over the continually increasing cost of the F-14. As the number of projected F-14 buys was continually reduced by the Navy, there was less projected program revenue that could absorb the company's overhead costs and hence the product cost continued to escalate. There was a crying need for overhead reduction. Most of the overhead reductions had to come from reduced indirect staff which meant layoffs across the board.

The most positive activity that took place during O'Brien's tour was the award of the Air Force E-8 Joint Surveillance Target Attack Radar System (JSTARS) Program. Unfortunately, this program would require a continued investment for some period before it could begin to produce a profit. This investment was one the company could hardly afford to make in a period when management was trying to improve the company's overall financial position.

John O'Brien was only able to watch as the financial indicators of the company were all heading in the wrong direction. As president, O'Brien could do little to quickly change the financial situation. He could and did take many steps to cut operating costs. The McKinsey driven cost reduction program was one of his first attempts to streamline internal operations. Revenues were increasing but with the constant fight to hold on to the F-14 program Grumman was losing in excess of $1 million on every F-14 delivered. In a company the size of Grumman, O'Brien knew that any changes he could implement would likely take years to pay dividends. Many of the factors driving the company's financial downward spiral had been put into place years before with flawed strategic business decisions. Let me illustrate a few of the financial factors as they were recorded during the O'Brien period as President and later as Chairman. The charts will clearly illustrate that only during O'Brien's tour as Chairman was he able to realize any significant change. For the most part, that change was only able to slow down or stop the hemorrhaging of the company's liquidity.

Revenue had been rising steadily when O'Brien took over as president in 1986 as shown in the chart below.

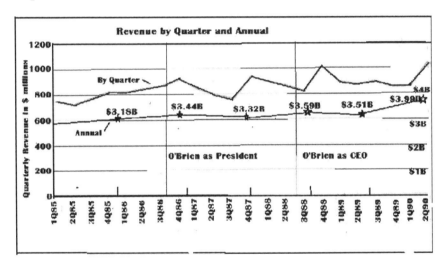

Revenue fluctuations began in late 1986 and continued through the end of O'Brien's term as CEO. Fluctuations are not unusual and are normally caused by changes made to the Navy's annual quantity buys of aircraft due to budget limitations.

Long term debt had been rising when O'Brien took over as President. As CEO he was able to significantly reduce the rise in debt, but he was not able to lower it.

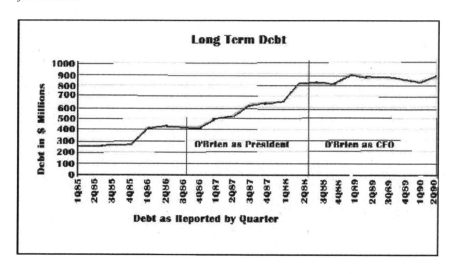

A high debt to-equity ratio generally means that a company has been aggressive in financing its growth with debt. This can result in volatile earnings as a result of the additional interest expense. When debt is used to finance increased operations, leading to a high debt to equity ratio, a company can potentially generate more earnings than it would have without this outside financing. If this were to increase earnings a greater amount than the cost of the debt (interest), the shareholders would benefit as more earnings are being spread among the same number of shareholders. However, the cost of this debt financing may outweigh the return generated on the debt through investment and business activities, becoming too much for the company to handle. This can lead to bankruptcy which would leave the shareholders with nothing.

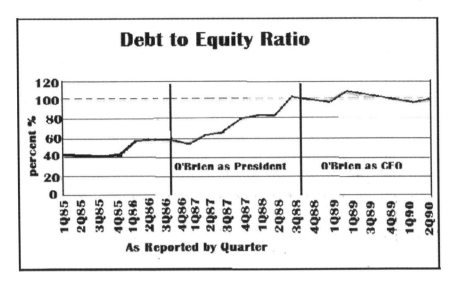

The operating income to interest coverage ratio shown below is a very telling indicator of company financial health.

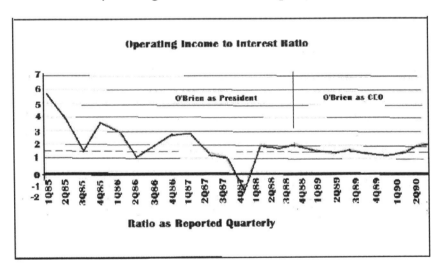

The lower this ratio becomes, the more the company is burdened with its debt expense. If the company's interest coverage ratio is 1.5 or lower, its ability to meet interest expenses becomes questionable. If the interest coverage ratio drops below 1.0, it indicates the company is not generating sufficient revenue to satisfy interest expenses. Between 1985 and 1990, this dangerous situation happened several times. O'Brien was able to stabilize this ratio as CEO but all during his tenure as CEO it hovered around the 1.5 value.

Operating margins are of course a big indicator of company performance and drive the calculation of company value.

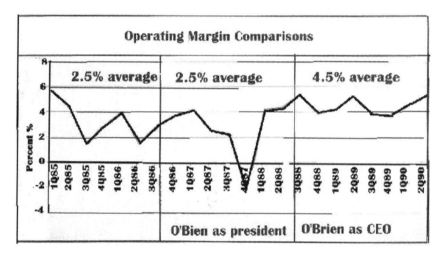

Before O'Brien took over as President, operating margins were steadily falling. He was able to stabilize this fall for much of his presidential term averaging a margin of 2.5%. As CEO he was able to raise that margin to an average of 4.5%.

Another primary indicator of the value of a company is the stock price to book value ratio.

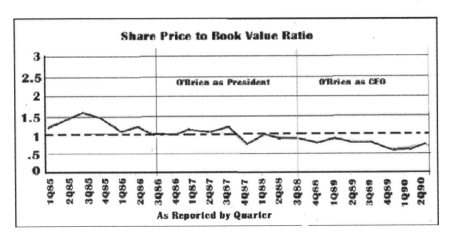

Some analysts believe that a company should always trade at a value higher than the book value of the company. This would create a price to book value of greater than 1.0. This is an area where John O'Brien can't claim much success for his efforts since the ratio was less than 1.0 during his entire term as President and CEO. Although not an exact indicator, if the price to book ratio is less than 1.0, it would indicate that the stock value is less than the liquidation value. In the financial community this situation would trigger the statement that the company is "worth more dead than it is alive," meaning that there is more value in liquidating the company's assets than in the stock value.

I must state again that most of these financial measures were deteriorating over the course of several years and it is nearly impossible to make significant improvements in any area in a short period of time unless there is a complete change in corporate financial strategy, structure and behavior.

What O'Brien was able to accomplish seems to be only a drop in the bucket toward what was needed to restore the financial health of Grumman. He should be given credit, however, for making some significant improvements. In aviation language, as a pilot, if your aircraft is in an uncontrolled spin and heading for the ground at a rapidly increasing speed, it takes a series of properly implemented actions to make a safe recovery. There were simply too many instruments spinning out of control for O'Brien to make all of the right moves. He did manage to stabilize the flight of the company in some areas but the seemingly constant battle against big odds with the F-14 was seriously hurting the company.

O'Brien began implementation of his geographical plan which began to take its toll on the company's Long Island population. He established a JSTARS production facility in Lake Charles, Louisiana. He opened a clean electronics manufacturing facility in Benton, Pa. He put the facility that Senator Byrd had requested in West Virginia, and he increased the company's presence in Houston, Texas. O'Brien never realized his plan to move more than half of the company's employees off of Long Island, but that objective was realized two years after his departure as shown in the chart below.

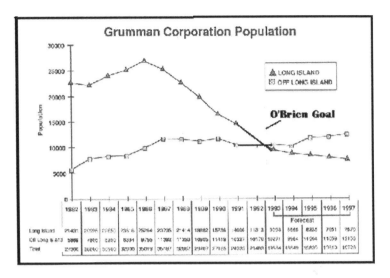

This chart was created in 1993, the years following being projections without any knowledge of the future take-over by Northrop. Unfortunately, the chart illustrates that most of the change that led to this location crossover resulted from reductions in the Long Island work force rather than from major increases in the off Long Island population. As this book was being written, the Long Island population plan called for fewer than 300 employees to remain on Long Island.

In an attempt to deal with the need for process change throughout the company, O'Brien jumped on the Total Quality Program bandwagon. The Malcolm Baldridge Total Quality Program was gaining interest throughout the country and was one of those movements that got the endorsement of the Defense Department. It was essentially mandated to every defense contractor. The concept of this program was to take individual operating processes within the company and turn the evaluation of those processes over to groups of employees. The theory was that the rank and file employees knew where the inefficiencies were located and they were in the best position to make recommendations for process corrections.

I believe that nearly all of the management within the company was originally skeptical about this approach, but as the program progressed, most became believers.

O'Brien chose not to appoint a Corporate President during his reign as CEO and that may have been a serious mistake. There were simply too many issues that needed attention and despite his use of his corporate staff, he was simply unable to maintain the proper focus on the important issues. O'Brien's passion about the geo-politics of Grumman's New York location became nearly an obsession. He knew that without the continued revenue stream of the F-14 program there was little possibility that he could right Grumman's financial ship. He worked tirelessly with the company's Washington office to gain support from every possible area of the defense political system. Perhaps this effort would eventually lead to his downfall.

O'Brien had previously made the Long Island business leaders aware of his feelings about the future of the area in terms of continuing defense business. His leadership in the area was a factor in the creation of Aeropac, an association of Long Island business leaders formed to gain the maximum amount of support from politicians from all areas of the country that were highly involved in the defense business. Many of the leaders of these member companies were also subcontractors or suppliers to Grumman so they had more than a passing interest in Grumman's future success. O'Brien made the fatal mistake of permitting his business relationships with Aeropac members to intermingle with his personal relationships. The Grumman Board of directors were made aware of this uncomfortable situation and asked for O'Brien's resignation in 1990.

Chapter Three

You Never Know About Political Networking

I've described our involvement with Texas politicians in Chapter One to provide a comparison with the lack of political support that Grumman was receiving from its own political leaders. The power of political networking cannot be overestimated. The following examples clearly demonstrate how effective political networking can be when practiced skillfully.

It isn't always possible to determine exactly how one might benefit from political networking, especially when it appears to have no absolute relationship with current business opportunities. Astute management requires that this type of networking be done with an eye on both short term operational needs and longer term strategic possibilities. Two examples illustrate this point.

During our dealing with the construction of a facility for a segment of our Space Division in Houston, I had several dealings with the Mayor of Houston, Kathy Whitmire. She was the first woman to be elected to the Houston city government becoming Mayor in 1986. I began dealing with her in 1990 and at her request made several visits to Houston to network with other Texas politicians who were interested in Grumman's presence there.

With the tremendous power base of the Texas political delegation in national politics, one might feel that dealing with the Mayor of a major Texas city had little to offer. I remembered the Lew Evans concept that in politics, you never want to make enemies, so if the Mayor of Houston wanted to be involved, that was fine with me.

We received a call in May of 1991 from the Mayor's office indicating that The Queen of England and her husband, Prince Charles, were visiting Houston on May 23rd. Grumman was being asked to attend a special lunch that was planned in their honor at the Johnson Space Center on that day. We purchased five tickets to the affair and arrived in Houston on the day of the event. We entered the reception area at the Johnson Space Center and proceeded to register for the luncheon affair. When I reached the registration table, I was told that I was to be seated at the head table as the guest of Mayor Whitmire, and I was to go to a specific room for a briefing.

I proceeded to the assigned room as directed assuming that I would be part of a large number of people that often are part of a long head table. When I entered the room, to my surprise there were only five other people there. I was informed that the Queen's table would consist of seven people. I was to be the guest of Mayor Whitmire; Robert Gilruth, the former head of the Johnson Space center and his wife Georgene; and another couple who I do not remember. The seventh person of course was to be the Queen. We were given some protocol instructions and led into the main reception room. The Queen's table was set for seven people and name cards were properly placed at each seat. That is when I received my second surprise. I was to be seated immediately to the right of the Queen, with Robert Gilruth immediately to her left. The other four guests were appropriately seated around the table.

During my career at Grumman there had been several occasions when I was to be in the company of people of significant status. These were usually members of Congress, Senators or other political figures. When these events were planned I had always been thoroughly briefed by my staff, so I could carry on an intelligent conversation. This was to be a new experience. The Queen was apparently in the United States to buy some horses. Her group had been in Kentucky and they were making a stop-over in Houston. I knew nothing at all about horses except that they usually smelled awful and could usually be seen running around a track. I also knew very little about the politics of the United Kingdom, and nothing about the Royal Family. What was I to do? I had no choice but to wing it, as I had done many times. But this time it was the Queen!

We all took our seats and the Queen and her husband were introduced to the crowd as they entered the room to be seated. As directed, the Queen sat immediately to my left. Prince Charles was seated at a second head table. Her Majesty was graciously introduced to each of us at her table and we were seated. From all that I had read or heard about the royal family, I expected the Queen to be a stogy lady, wearing an out-of-period hat that probably had a slightly moldy odor. Well, she did wear a hat, but that was about my only expectation she met. She was totally gracious to everyone at the table. She led the conversation at all times and made all of us feel very comfortable in her presence. She worked the table with the grace and skill of a seasoned socialite. She changed the subject regularly and made the forty minute lunch seem like an instant.

When the luncheon was over and the Queen left the room, I had a chance to have some light conversation with Robert Gilruth, whom I had known, but never met, during the Apollo Program. Gilruth talked of his memories of his friendship with Lew Evans. Both Evans and his wife and Gilruth and his wife had been friends for many years during the heart of the space program. Gilruth's wife had passed away years earlier and of course Lew Evans had passed in

1972. As fate would have it, Georgene Evans eventually had married Gilruth and it was she that accompanied him at this luncheon. When the event was over I realized what a truly small world it was.

More important than the event itself was the reality that relationships, such as the political connections we had made in Texas, were a very large part of a company's ability to survive in our very competitive environment. It reminded me then, as it still does today, how Important John O'Brien's mission was to place Grumman into a better and more advantageous political environment. I never believed that this lunch with the Queen of England would bring any positive result for Grumman. I will, however, always remember it as an opportunity that arose from a solid relationship with the Mayor of Houston.

The second example also involves the relationship with the Mayor of Houston. I received a call from Mayor Whitmire indicating that Prince Felipe of Spain was going to be visiting Houston the following week as part of his royal duties to promote Spanish business. The Prince was well educated at Georgetown University and a pilot in the Spanish military. As a pilot, Mayor Whitmire thought I might make a fine host for the Prince at a private luncheon she had planned. I agreed to host the luncheon. Not knowing much about Spanish politics, I asked members of Grumman's International group to accompany Clyde Stover and me to Houston.

The luncheon was held in a very private facility with very few people in attendance. The Prince was very young and also very shy. We discussed a few aviation related subjects where I took the opportunity to brief him on several of the Grumman products that might eventually be of interest to his government.

In thanks for my hosting the luncheon, the prince presented me with a sterling silver letter opener which was engraved with his royal identity. I believe I presented him with a model of the Grumman OV-1 Mohawk, an aircraft he apparently had flown.

At that point the luncheon with the prince was over and, I thought, gone forever. On June 19, 2014 as I was writing this book, I suddenly took notice of a newscast in the background. King Juan Carlos of Spain had just abdicated the thrown and a new King was crowned in Spain. Guess who? Yes, it was Prince Felipe the new King of Spain, the same Felipe that I had hosted for lunch more than 20 years earlier. This young, shy, good looking Spaniard was now the new King of Spain.

Would either the Queen of England or the new King of Spain even remember these two events? I doubt it. But to me it is representative of how and why it is always wise in the business world to keep all of your political options open. These two events fall into the category of "you never know" when future paths may cross so never make political enemies.

On both of these Texas events, I included a marketing representative from Grumman's International Division. My contacts with the Queen or the future King were certainly less important than the contacts made by our people with their attending staff members. International business always required that a company have contacts that could "open doors" to the right people for future business dealings. These are the strategic opportunities I mentioned earlier.

Chapter Four

Understanding Grumman's Early Difficulties

When I completed my service term as a Second Lieutenant in the US Army in 1959, I worked at The Hazeltine Corporaton in Little Neck, New York. I called this a "hard core" company and I selected it because engineering was a hands-on job there. Engineers started with a tool box and were assigned a work bench in addition to a desk. I quickly realized that this was actually the best way to practice engineering, put your designs on paper and then take some parts and actually build the "breadboard" yourself.

Things worked well for me at Hazeltine and within a year I was moved to their research center in Plainview, New York. That was also a fine experience, working with people I knew were much more intelligent than me. It made me work harder to keep up, but keeping up was not my style, I wanted to excel at what I did so I was always the first one in to work in the morning and the last one to leave at night. I used my work ethic to make up for my possible intellectual weaknesses. My advancement continued at Hazeltine, but I wanted something broader in scope than the circuit design work that I was doing.

There was plenty of opportunity on Long island at that time and I started to look at Grumman. My research on the company showed me a company that was different in many ways. One factor that played a big part in my decision to join Grumman was their internal promotion policy. Nearly all of the managers and executives in Grumman were people who had started at the bottom and moved up in the ranks because of their capability. I thought, "this is a company where performance pays off and that excites me." I was young and benefits were not important to me at that time, but the quality of the people was important and I wanted this to be my career company.

Occasionally I would walk through the executive area of plant five, called "mahogany row," where the company's leaders were officed. Most of those leaders were in some way connected to the founders of the company who had earned their positions through hard work and dedication. As I got more familiar with many of these executives, I realized that they were not necessarily brilliant in their fields, but they were good at what they did and they knew how to manage people. The success of the company at that time was proof of their management capability. The products that they built were proof that their system worked.

Grumman was essentially a Navy contractor and had developed strong relationship with Navy officials over the years. The reason for these close relationships, of course, was that the products that were delivered to the Navy were very effective war fighting machines that got the job done. Grumman built a good product and the company stood behind its products and its customers.

It was also an era where the government procurement system was fairly simple. If the Navy needed more airplanes, a simple phone call to the Grumman leaders would make it happen. If, on the other hand, Grumman needed a little more business to keep its costs down, a phone call in the other direction would make that happen.

In the early 1960's Grumman made its first entry into the space business, winning the Orbiting Astronomical Observatory (OAO). As George Skurla points out in his book **Inside The iron Works**, the top brass of Grumman were not enthusiastic about entering the space business because it wasn't obvious that the company could make any money from these programs. Grumman had become comfortable with the Navy's procurement practices and management didn't want to take on big risk programs and put the company's profit performance at risk.

Despite these cautions, Lew Evans, President of the company at the time decided to move forward in Space. The 1960's was a benchmark period for Grumman, but also a period that set the stage for many problems in years to come. Grumman won the Lunar Module program and the F-14 fighter program in the same period. NASA procurement policies were fair to participating companies but the F-14 required a significant investment by the company and fixed pricing practices put the company in a dangerous investment position. The Navy's new Total Package Procurement approach to contracting on the F-14 program had never before been tried. Traditionally the government would procure the engines and much of the other government furnished equipment (GFE), and supply that hardware to the aircraft designers. The F-14 program would be different. The prime contractor was responsible for the total package, taking all of the risk off of the government and placing it all on themselves. The F-14 was a great morale win for Grumman, but it was also the start of Grumman's financial slide.

The company's financial problems initially caused by the F-14 procurement rules was apparently one of the reasons that Jack Bierwirth was brought into the company and made its financial Vice President. Bierwirth had developed solid relationships with the big banks and he was able to convince them to continue Grumman's line of credit. When Lew Evans died unexpectedly, it was necessary for then CEO Clint Towl to move Bierwirth into the presidency to fill the void left by Evans.

Clint Towl's retirement, perhaps earlier than expected, accelerated Bierwith's upward mobility to the Chairman's position. Towl apparently recognized that the solid relationships that Grumman had with the Navy brass were being weakened by the continued arguments about the F-14 cost situation. Towl apparently gave Bierwirth a clear mandate to begin diversifying the company into areas outside purely aerospace businesses, and Bierwirth took that mandate seriously. The problem was that Bierwirth was also apparently told that to be successful in non-defense businesses, he had to keep the high cost aerospace technology people (the engineers) away from those businesses. That attitude placed an invisible barrier between Bierwirth and most of the company that had been raised in the aircraft technology business.

During most of Jack Bierwirth's tenure as CEO, the company's aircraft related products continued to move along fairly well except for the financial problems on the F-14. Bierwirth surged ahead with his diversification program only to find the results of those efforts were incurring additional financial losses for the company. According to some sources, these losses totaled more than $500 million.

The one, single incident that brought serious criticism to Bierwirth was his decision to sell the Gulfstream business. Like most Grumman employees, I could never understand why this move was made. The Gulfstream, to many of us, was a well known, high quality, trademark product of the company. It wasn't until I started doing the research for this book and was given information about the events that took place at the time of the sale, that I changed my mind about directing blame only at Bierwirth.

In his book **Inside The Iron Works,** George Skurla gave his version of the events that led up to the sale of the Gulfstream. There is, however, more to that story that I feel needs to be told. Perhaps these new facts will lead us to place less blame on Jack Bierwirth for that action.

During the early 1970's, sales of the Gulfstream aircraft to domestic companies was falling off significantly. The rapidly increasing cost of fuel was driving big US companies away from the larger gas guzzling airplanes. The foreign market however was building rapidly. Every Middle Eastern Sheik and African dictator had to have the newest and most luxurious aircraft. The Gulfstream filled that need completely. Doing business in that foreign environment was completely different than our domestic market. Every buyer had a stream of agents through which every sale had to pass. There was essentially no way to enter these foreign markets without paying your way in with fees and commissions. It was just the way it was at the time.

The Lockheed bribery scandals in the mid 1970's created a series of investigations by the Securities and Exchange

Commission into the practices being used by US companies to sell their products overseas. It was determined that Lockheed made payments of more than $300 million to various foreign organizations as entry fees to their markets. When the SEC investigations revealed that there were more than 400 US companies that had admitted to making similar payments, although smaller in size, the issue became national in stature. The result was the creation of a Senate Select Committee, headed by Senator Frank Church.

The Lockheed scandals became a well known, international incident. The former Prime Minister of Japan, Kokuei Tanaka was arrested and the scandal led to the downfall of Prime Minister Tukeo Miki of Japan. This scandal also resulted in the resignation from all government positions of Prince Bernhard of the Netherlands.

The Church Committee called Joe Gavin and Jack Bierwirth to testify about possible payments made by Grumman to Iranian officials to open markets for the company's F-14. The committee also probed fees and commissions paid by Grumman as entry into foreign markets for the Gulfstream aircraft. What is rarely or never printed about these hearings was the fact that nearly every foreign market required entry by payments of fees and commissions in order to do business in that country. American companies were in a quandary because business in the United States was slowing down and the foreign markets were the only place to turn for additional sales. If entry fees were required they were simply paid as a cost of doing business.

Grumman emerged from the Church hearings without any criminal or civil charges. Grumman was, however, served with a permanent injunction which was in essence a warning to stay clear of doing business with foreign agents. This essentially closed the foreign markets to Grumman for the sale of Gulfstream aircraft. There were many nearly completed green aircraft on the production line with no foreign customers able to buy them.

The result of the Church Committee hearings was the creation of the Foreign Corrupt Practices Act of 1977. The act incorporates a dual approach to discourage what they called foreign bribery. It imposes affirmative requirements upon users registered with the SEC to maintain detailed records and develop internal controls to insure that corporate assets are properly used. Secondly, the act creates civil liabilities and criminal penalties for any US company that makes illegal payments to foreign organizations or individuals. President Jimmy Carter signed the act into law on December 19, 1977.

Because of the permanent injunction served to Grumman, the Board of Directors became nervous about foreign sales of the Gulfstream aircraft. Meanwhile the Gulfstream was in need of a major design upgrade and there was significant disagreement among the Directors of Gulfstream American on the design approach to that modification, even to the extent that some board members wanted to take the design outside of Grumman jurisdiction. This, of course, was completely unacceptable to Grumman. After all, the Gulfstream was a trademark product for the company, the thought of non-Grumman engineers designing the next generation aircraft was not realistic.

Meanwhile Allen Paulson offered to buy the company from Grumman. He felt that as a privately held company, he would not be subject to the rules of SEC oversight, which was probably not true.

Paulson's offer came at precisely the right time. Grumman's financial position was shaky and Bierwirth felt that Grumman needed the money. At the same time the Grumman Board had done an audit resulting from the Church Committee hearings and they were very skeptical of continuing business with foreign governments. Continuing with the Gulfstream was also going to require a significant investment in the next generation aircraft, an investment that Grumman could not afford at the time. Rather than face the continued doubt of the Board of Directors, Bierwirth decided to accept Paulson's offer and he sold Gulfstream American to Paulson for $52 million.

At this point in history, the Gulfstream story shifts to a lesson in entrepreneurship. Allen Paulson was born in a small town in Iowa in 1922. In 1941 he became an aircraft mechanic for Trans World Airways earning 30 cents an hour. He served in the Army from 1943 until 1945. In 1951 he formed the California Airmotive Corporation with the objective to convert surplus passenger planes into freight carrying airplanes.

In 1970 he changed the nature of that company into American Jet industries which converted piston powered airplanes into propjets.

In 1972 Grumman merged with light aircraft manufacturer American Aviation and merged the Gulfstream aircraft operations with the small light aircraft of American Aviation to form Gulfstream American Corp.

In 1978 Paulson bought Gulfstream American from Grumman for what amounted to around $52 million. The background of that purchase is described above.

Paulson changed the name of the company to Gulfstream Aerospace, expanded its facilities and pared back its product mix, shedding the light aircraft products. He then sold the business to Chrysler Corporation for $648 million in 1985.

Chrysler eventually realized that its core competence did not lie in the aircraft business. Paulson, partnered with Forstmann, Little & Co. and bought the company back from Chrysler for $850 million in 1990.

After continual improvements in the Gulfstream aircraft design and the continual upgrades in its models, Gulfstream Aerospace was sold later in the 1990's to General Dynamics for $5.3 billion. The company at that time had a $4.1 billion backlog of 129 airplanes. Employment at the company when it was last sold was over 11,500 employees.

The Gulfstream story is of course a story of American entrepreneurship. But it is also another example of the difficulty of dealing with customers that are largely from the US Government. Company market plans are never firm due to constantly changing bureaucratic and political objectives. American corporations are required to make gigantic investments in technical developments and government production programs, with little promise of ever realizing acceptable returns on those investments. At the same time these companies are significantly restricted in their ability to market their products to foreign customers by rules established by the US Government. Is it any wonder that large commercial US companies shy away from doing business with their own Government due to regulations and restrictions that limit their profitability.

Jack Bierwirth took a lot of flack internally, not only for the sale of the Gulfstream, but also for some of his other diversification efforts. His purchase of the Flexible Bus Company from the Rohr Company in 1978 was an indication why it was a mistake to keep the company's technical brains away from the non-defense products. The busses were originally designed with a technical flaw that most certainly would have been detected by the company's aircraft design team if they had been consulted. Of course after the problem became a company buster, the aerospace structures people were called in to suggest a repair.

Bierwirth re-organized the entire company into nine divisions under a common corporate management structure. As the corporate CEO he appointed George Skurla as corporate president in 1985 but Skurla was already 64 years old and by company rules was required to retire at the age of 65 in 1986. Bierwirth appointed John O'brien corporate President to replace Skurla. When Bierwirth retired in 1988 he appointed O'Brien CEO.

O'Brien took over a company that was fraught with problems. O'Brien who, like most other Grumman executives, had moved up through the ranks of the company, believed that his previous positions had permitted him to clearly understand the problems of the company and therefore he was in a good position to solve these problems. He didn't want to be faced with a situation that he had seen before where the CEO and President often were on different sides of critical issues so he held both the CEO and Chief Operating Officer titles.

O'Brien had moved up through the company with long term experience in government contracting and business strategy. He believed that if Grumman was to survive as an aerospace leader, the company could not do it from its Long Island location. He also recognized that the age old relationships that the Grumman founders had established with Navy decision makers were no longer going to prevail since national politics was now playing a much more important role in the defense procurement process. O'Brien began to get very active in the political process and became even more convinced that Grumman had accrued no political favors in Washington due to the relatively weak standing of its congressional delegation.

O'Brien took action to implement his relocation program by locating a plant in East Benton, Pa. Activities related to the building of this plant were among the first that drew O'Brien into an uncomfortable political posture. He later built a plant in Clarksburg, West Virginia which I describe elsewhere in this book. O'Brien's biggest program location move was his decision to move the production of the E-8 JSTARS program to Lake Charles, Louisiana where thousands of employees would be involved in that effort. He also expanded the company's presence in Texas with his effort to locate a portion of the Space Division's work to that area (also described elsewhere). Every one of these geographic moves was consistent with his strategy to build a strong political support base for the company away from Long Island.

O'Brien, like executives who came before him, recognized that his ability to re-direct the company back to its core capability in aerospace would be hampered by its current financial situation. Although company revenues appeared to be at a nearly all time high, the stock had reached its all time low of $13 per share. The company had accumulated a debt of nearly $1 billion which was rated at BBB and under threat of again being downgraded to "junk bond" status. The company was courting bankruptcy with a likely decline in revenue over the next four years of nearly 30%.

Early in his first year as president, O'Brien asked me to form a small team and take a quick look at Fairchild Republic. This Farmingdale, Long Island company had a proud history of building aircraft for the Air Force, but at this point it was close to being dissolved. O'Brien was probably taking this step as a sign of good faith to the local political leaders who were concerned about Long Island's declining defense business. O'Brien had already made his feeling known publically about the future of Long Island. O'Brien felt that perhaps there was some little spark of business left at Republic that would benefit Grumman.

Years earlier, Republic Aviation had been purchased by the Fairchild Corporation. Its most recent success was being awarded the contract to develop the Air Force A-10 Warthog aircraft that first flew in May of 1972. At this juncture the A-10 was still in operation but production had been terminated. Republic's last gasp effort to stay afloat was the T-46A trainer for the Air Force. The company closed its doors when, for budgetary reasons, the Air Force failed to take the program into production.

When my team arrived at Republic, there was little left to examine. It was obvious to me the only reason we were even taking the time to look was probably to satisfy some local political pressure to try to help the Long Island economy. Grumman had its low speed wind tunnel on the Republic site, but that could continue as a separate entity. There was little asset value in Republic's remains and there were some significant environmental factors that raised question as to the value of the property on which many of the facilities were located. Grumman's decision was not to proceed further with any evaluation.

Normally the story would end here, but not so fast. Jump ahead to 2013. There are still 346 A-10's in operation by the

Air Force. Half are in regular service and half are used by the Air National Guard. The Air Force has decided to keep the airplane in operation through 2018 with the award of a Life Cycle Program Support (TLPS) Program. The contract language for this program calls for the possible upgrade to the plane's systems in the future. Ironically, the $24 million contract was awarded to-----Northrop Grumman.

Chapter Five

The Doctor Arrives

Almost immediately after the Board accepted the resignation of John O'Brien, they appointed Dr. Renso Caporali as Grumman's new CEO. Dr. Caporali was well known throughout Grumman, having started with the company in 1959 and spending his entire career there. Caporali had received his Bachelors and Masters degrees from Clarkson College. He went on to receive his Masters in Aeronautical Engineering and a Masters of Arts in Aerospace Engineering from Princeton University. He received an AIAA fellowship award and received his Ph.D in Aeronautical Engineering from Princeton University. Caporali was also a licensed Professional Engineer and served in the Navy as a Lt.CDR. and P-2 pilot. Grumman had also sent Caporali to Harvard University to complete the Advanced Management Program. The initial announcement appointing Caporali as the new CEO indicated that the appointment was temporary. The Board would do a complete search before making any permanent appointment. Those of us who were fairly close to Caporali knew very well that the Board had picked the best person for the job and this would indeed be a permanent assignment.

When Caporali was later announced officially as Grumman's new CEO, I was reminded of a conversation I had years earlier with George Skurla. Skurla had just received word that he was being returned to New York to head the Product Engineering Department. I was in Florida briefing him on some of the key engineering issues at that time and we were having a casual conversation about Grumman while having dinner at Skurla's favorite burger joint. Skurla indicated that his tour at Cape Kennedy had been an interesting experience in many ways. One thing that had impressed him about NASA was the number of Ph.D's they employed. He indicated that no matter where he went, there were Ph.D's in charge. Grumman, he said, has few if any Ph.D's. He bragged about Dr. Ralph Tripp as one of the few that had achieved that status and felt that Grumman needed more Ph.D's in key positions.

Now for the first time, Grumman had a Ph.D as its corporate leader. But Caporali's task was no longer an engineering challenge. It was the daunting task of turning the company around financially. Caporali had seen the effects of a CEO trying to do it all himself and he was not going to fall victim to that mistake. He quickly appointed Bob Myers as president and then went outside the company and hired Robert Anderson, who had been the Vice Chairman and CFO of Firestone Tire and Rubber Company. Caporali apparently believed that a new set of eyes was necessary to resolve the many financial issues that were facing the company. Caporali had visions of a slightly different Grumman but he knew that to even begin the task of moving the company forward he would first have to improve the company's dire financial condition.

Media reports about Caporali indicated that he had no plans to change the direction of the company from its current path. Those who knew him, however, knew that could not have been farther from the truth. He knew that company revenue would hold fairly constant for another year or so, but after that sales would start to drop as the A-6 and F-14 programs came to an end. He had the new JSTARS program, but that was still in development and decent profits would not be realized from that program for a couple of years. Caporali may have been a brilliant engineer but he also knew a little about finance. If he was going to change the company's financial situation, it was going to require some major cuts in the workforce and some rather significant changes to the operating processes of the company.

Caporali's management style was going to be quite different from his predecessor. His appointment of Bob Myers as President was the first indicator that he had no intentions of pulling all of the strings himself but would rather get things done through his organization. Some had defined

O'Brien as a man who used the "bully pulpit" to get things done and, to some extent, that was probably true. O'Brien also was faced with a daunting task and that was his way of keeping things moving. Caporali didn't have the personality for that leadership style. The single most important issue facing the new CEO was the massive company debt. Without fixing that problem there was no chance of thinking about growth. Much of the company debt was in long term bonds and those bonds were paying unusually high interest rates. Unfortunately the only way to fix that without paying a premium was to wait until the bonds expired and to pay them off either by re-financing (which Caporali refused to do) or by making the hard decisions to pay the debt with money generated by operational savings.

Caporali took several steps to start his financial recovery program. He initiated an Executive Review Board which consisted of executives representing the financial, technology and business areas of the company. I was asked to chair this Board and our task was to review all new ventures being proposed by the different division of the company, to insure that they were cost effective businesses, and represented good shareholder value. Both Caporali and Myers held positions on the board but they chose to let the board come forth with recommendations. Their role would be to make the final decision based on board findings.

Bob Anderson instituted a Performance Improvement Program (PIP) which required each of the organizations within the company to make significant improvements in their operating financial performance. This long term program would result in eventual reductions in facilities, processes and employment.

Results were starting to take hold from the Total Quality Program. Caporali was initially skeptical about this program but quickly realized the benefits of this program and threw his support behind it. This effort worked hand in hand with the PIP program, making changes in those processes within the company that would lead to better efficiency.

Furthering Caporali's objective to get things done through his management organization, he established the company's first strategic management conference, held off site at the Arrowwood Conference Center in Rye Brook, New York. This three-day, working conference was designed to look at the company's critical issues and have working groups of management personnel bring forth recommendations for changes in direction. Caporali set the tone for this conference by putting the facts on the table about the condition of the company and the opportunities that were available in the future. He also made it clear that our future success was in the hands of all of us. By his leadership style, Caporali made us all feel like we all had some "skin in the game," a step that had a noticeable effect on the speed with which company changes were to be made.

At the beginning of Caporali's term of leadership, most of the revenue producing programs were in fairly good shape permitting almost immediate payoff from any significant improvements in operating efficiency. He knew, however, that there was a time limit on this revenue situation. The A-6 program was coming to an end and although the F-14 fight was ongoing, that would eventually also come to an end.

The situation with the F-14 needed continued attention since the budget battle would take place every year. Caporali needed to attend to that situation in two ways. The rather aggressive approach that had been taken in recent years to protect the F-14 was coupled to some strong political activity where some key people on the Washington scene had become annoyed at Grumman's aggressive actions. Caporali had to insure that we continued to make our point in favor of the F-14 over the F-18, but Grumman had to take immediate steps to repair its image in Washington.

As part of his personal efforts to create a new company image in Washington, Caporali testified before a senate committee investigating defense industry conversion. Even back in those days, most of the activities of both the House and Senate involved hearings on whatever subject seemed to surface that needed investigation. No action was usually taken from these hearings but the hearing went on. (Seems like nothing has changed in that arena in 20 years.)

In his testimony Caporali stated that "The defense industry diversification efforts of the 1970's were notably unsuccessful. From watches to coffins to subway cars and solar panels, companies got into businesses they knew nothing about with predictable results. In most cases, companies were trying to break into markets that already had sufficient suppliers. In others, they were offering technologies no one wanted.

"By trying to become something we'll never be, we're wasting what we already are"Caporali told the senators.

This reminded me of a statement made by Norm Augustine, CEO of Martin Marietta. Regarding diversification he stated; "the history of the defense industry diversification efforts has been untarnished by success."

Caporali's statement about diversification had specific meaning to him because the financial situation he inherited was mostly caused by past diversification attempts that had failed. Caporali went on to tell the Senate committee that the defense industry had developed a tremendous pool of talent that was available to help solve many of the country's complicated problems. "Because of the risk involved, raising sufficient private investment capital for such projects is impossible. Industry cannot tackle these projects alone. A government mandate creates a market for the skills the defense industry already has in place; and I believe that creating a market is the best way government can effect defense conversion."

Caporali went on to give his opinion that the world is far too unstable for us to assume that military build-ups are a thing of the past. Government actions in support of new mandates of this type would help preserve the capability of the industry to respond if future needs dictated.

"…A number of things will help effect a defense conversion. Breaking down the walls between commercial and military development and procurement; better investment tax credits and a more supportive export policy are actions that can be taken. But given the magnitude of the problem, all of these things are secondary to what I believe is the real answer: that government must create the markets."

Caporali got personally involved with the F-14 discussions in Washington, but this time he was not only the company CEO but also well known as one of the key designers of that aircraft and its weapon systems. His ability to present the technical argument was unquestionable.

By the end of his first year as CEO, all of these efforts were starting to pay dividends. A fast way to examine the progress made is to re-examine the same curves shown earlier to describe the O'Brien and pre O'Brien eras.

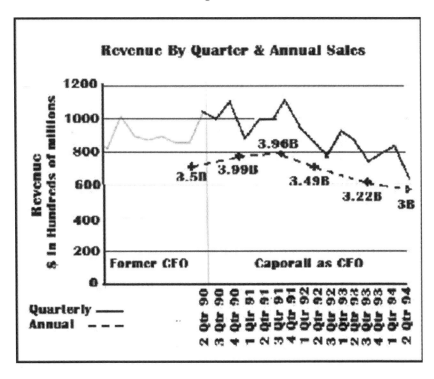

Revenues were holding at about the levels of the previous years as expected with projections for future years declining significantly. This set the time line for needed future changes.

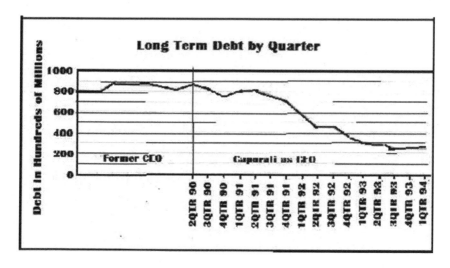

Long term debt in the first year was reduced by more than $100 million but the following years reduced it to nearly zero by the time the company was sold.

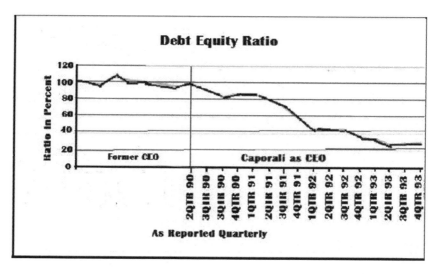

The debt to equity ratio in the first two years of his term was significantly reduced by 60%.

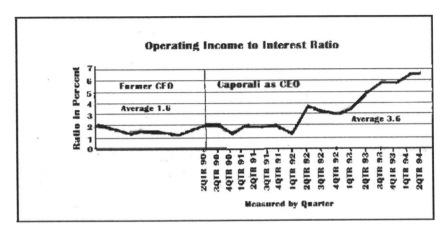

Of significant importance, the income to interest ratio was brought up above the 1.5 level which indicated that the company was no longer in danger of liquidation status.

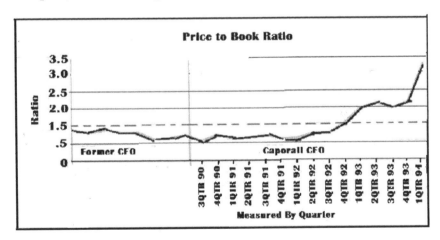

The price to book value ratio took a little longer to fix but it eventually moved above the danger zone.

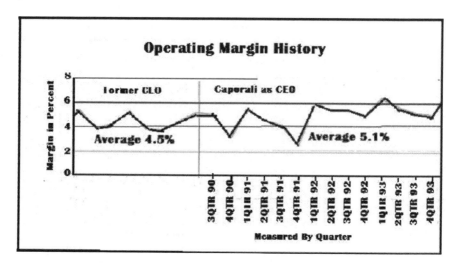

Operating profits were starting to increase as a result of operational cuts. Caporali brought the margins above 6% and averaged slightly above 5.1% during his time in office.

One financial analyst included the following in his analysis of Grumman at the time.

"Under Caporali's stewardship, Grumman experienced wholesale changes. The company's debt was trimmed by 60%, payroll was also reduced significantly. Grumman's headquarters staff was cut in half and the company began to look forward to growth."

When the devastating news came about the end of the F-14 program things were just starting to look up for Grumman, but the F-14 loss quickly changed that picture. As I stated in the introduction to this book, Caporali immediately set things in motion to develop a new strategy for the future of the company.

He directed that we establish a management team consisting of Bob Denien, Executive Vice President of the Aircraft Systems Group, me, and Richard Anderson, Corporate Vice President for Technology. He also directed that we bring in William Perry's company, Global Technology Partners to oversee our activities and decisions. Perry had served as Under Secretary of Defense for Research and Engineering from 1977 to 1981. Perry had assembled a group of experts who understood the ins and outs of the defense industry and also were experienced in government operations. We didn't expect to actually get Bill Perry himself, but he was the leader of the team that worked hand in hand with our study team, reviewing our findings on a weekly basis. We code-named this study the "Project X Studies."

Since the study might eventually evolve into some detailed evaluations of the corporate finances of several other companies, Bob Anderson, Grumman's CFO suggested that we also bring in Goldman Sachs, a company that had extensive experience in bringing together companies through mergers and acquisitions. The McKinsey group was also still available to us following our cost cutting studies in the previous years. We felt that the McKinsey old timers would be a good source to review our financial conclusions. The presence of these high level consultants would also help assure the objectivity of our work.

The study was designed in two distinct parts which were conducted in parallel. The first part of the study was directed at evaluating the ability of Grumman to combine with other companies in the electronics system integration business to retain the Grumman core competence in that area. The second part of the study was designed to evaluate if there were any possible partners that would keep Grumman and a partner in one of the key positions with regard to remaining a prime defense contractor.

The study group established a concept of 2+2=5, meaning that the most desirable combinations would be those where the combination of two companies would be greater than the sum of the individual parts of each company. There was no study technology that defined the basis of this type of analysis and it was decided that it would have to be a qualitative evaluation that could be layered on top of our quantitative studies.

It wasn't long after the devastating collapse of the F-14 that we reviewed all of our short and long term aircraft business opportunities. The results caused Caporali to make the very difficult decision that the days of Grumman performing in a prime contract role for a major aircraft program were over.

Grumman would take those steps necessary to restructure its operations to move in the direction of becoming the supplier of choice for high technology, integrated systems. In September of 1993 Grumman published its first Strategic Statement that set the stage for its future. The contents of that strategic statement are shown below.

Grumman Corporation
Strategic Statement
Published September, 1993

Grumman's current strong financial position is the result of a well-defined strategy for survival, change and growth. A continuing focus on shareholder value, through cash management and operating performance, has improved our position in the financial and investor markets, and provided access to capital for investment. Grumman is now positioned to leverage its strategy, technology and capabilities to address a challenging new marketplace and, through a series of carefully planned alliances, including acquisitions, undertake the changes needed to reposition the company for the future. These actions will be taken to both expand capabilities and market position, and to achieve the economies of scale needed for sustainable competitive advantages and increased shareholder value.

Aircraft design and manufacture have been the core of Grumman's business since its inception. Continuing production programs, together with an increasingly important series of upgrades and systems modifications, such as those performed on the F-14, E-2, EA-6. EF-111, A-6, OV-1 and C-2 have fueled our company over many years. Today however, the combined effect of the collapse of the Soviet Union and major, global economic shifts have triggered dramatic structural changes in the defense and aerospace industries. An almost complete absence of new starts, and prospects for minimal production over the next decade, have necessitated a rethinking of our strategy for the future. In the absence of strong Government support, sustaining the complete high performance airframe design and manufacturing capabilities associated with our traditional role as a vehicle prime contractor is clearly unaffordable. Conversely, we have no intention of stepping away from our Customers and the more than 1000 Grumman aircraft currently in service, since an important and sizeable market for upgrade and modification work on our own and others products continues to exist. Therefore, Grumman is initiating a restructuring of strategy and infrastructure which will emphasize, enhance and exploit our system design, development, production and integration capabilities, successfully developed and honed over the past three decades. We will compete on this basis, across all platforms, aircraft conversions, and aircraft components, each on the basis of best value for the individual customer. This position will allow Grumman to partner on any new aircraft program, and participate as a prime contractor on those programs which, like Joint Stars, depend upon the synthesis and integration of the on-board systems as the key to success.

Fundamental to this shift in strategic direction is an escalation in our emphasis of Electronic and Information Systems, linked together through the process and infrastructure of Systems Engineering and Integration. In addition to an extraordinary breath of systems experience, Grumman brings more than 30 years of Electronics design, manufacture and systems integration experience to this objective. Spanning the range from test equipment and trainers to the more recent combat electronics, this experience will be exploited to achieve dominance in surveillance systems and electronic warfare, and be leveraged to achieve a leading position in the areas of battle management systems and delivery platform integration.

Information Systems, both as an embedded element of defense systems and in stand-alone management and process systems, represents another major Grumman strength, one in which we have enjoyed significant success. In recent years, our credentials as an integrator of hardware and software solutions has facilitated expansion into non-defense federal markets. This experience and the leverage accruing from internal systems development provides a firm base from which to grow. Sales to federal, State and local government customers are a continuing focus but commercial endeavors that support these markets are also of growing interest.

Consistent with this central theme of integrating systems, Grumman has and will continue to focus on non-traditional applications of our primary raw material - advanced technology. Early on, our application of aerostructures technology led to a significant position in Ground Transportation, particularly in segments of the commercial vehicle and aluminum truck body market. This position is now being leveraged to achieve growth in the broader transportation market. In another arena, Grumman has established a lead technology position in advanced Energy Systems critical to such diverse emerging requirements as nuclear waste management, space propulsion, and high speed rail transport. Similar opportunities exist today for development and application of a broad range of technologies to problems of national and international scope including energy, environment, and health, to name but a few. In each case, prudent financial and operating parameters and market understanding will provide the framework to assure economic viability and competitive advantage.

In summary, Grumman's strategy is to grow by becoming the supplier of choice for high technology, integrated systems to defense, other government-related commercial customers. We will continually refine our technology, capabilities, and infrastructure to better match demands for agility and competitiveness, so as to further enhance operating performance and shareholder value. Carefully planned and executed acquisitions and other forms of alliances will become an integral part of our strategy, allowing Grumman to establish a position among the leaders over a range of markets, and thereby reducing dependence on individual segments of our overall market.

By this time Caporali and his management team had made significant progress in their attempt to put Grumman in a more attractive financial position. Some of us joked quietly that the doctor had stopped the hemorrhaging of cash within the company. He directed all of the company's decision makers to now begin to direct their thinking toward shareholder value added. Caporali had lived through the recent history of Grumman as we all had, and he believed that many of the decisions of the past that got the company into dire financial condition were made for reasons other than good financial logic. Caporali's position was well stated in a speech he made to defense company executives at the Electronics Industry Association annual conference in October 1993. Excerpts from that speech clearly tell Caporali's feelings.

"We in the defense industry today have fallen on hard times. Our markets are shrinking, we're faced with excess capacity, and there's a good deal of debate, particularly among politicians, about what defense companies ought to be doing to respond to such an environment. There has been a lot of talk among people in our industry about changes in the defense acquisition policy, and the need for more cooperation between industry and government. There has also been much talk about new requirements in the Middle East and analysis of a number of potential new markets.

"But as we assess the state of the industry and develop strategic plans for our companies, it seems that there is one important group that we may be overlooking, a group that has the absolute right to our attention. It's not the government, it's not the Department of Defense, it's not NASA. It's not the Navy, the Air Force or the Army. It's not our suppliers or our communities it's not even our employees. It's our Shareholders."

Chairman Caporali went on to discuss how political events make us feel that all of our companies are indispensable. He indicated that government tells us to take pride in the role that our products play in helping to maintain world order.

We tell ourselves that everything we have must be retained for that time when the world calls us again. He then goes on to cite some history.

"We say we must maintain a strong industrial base and that's good. But size doesn't equal strength. When we're tying up shareholder resources without reasonable hope of an appropriate return on their investment, we're doing the wrong thing. The result is a weakening, not strengthening of the industrial base we profess to be so concerned about.

"In a sense we have been duped by our own success, particularly in the electronics side of the defense industry. If you look at the airframe side of the defense business back in the 1950's and 60's there were any number of new starts. A new alloy would be developed, or a new engine and those things could yield aerodynamic advancements big enough and important enough to make a new aircraft program worthwhile. But technology has matured sufficiently that breakthroughs now are fewer and farther between. Today new aircraft starts of a specific type are 20, 25 years apart—and the gaps are growing."

"In the 1950's there were about 18 manufacturers of tactical aircraft. Today there are five. Within 10 years, the Department of Defense predicts there will be only two. It's difficult to do an analysis that suggests that the DOD is wrong."

Perhaps hinting at some Grumman past history, Caporali explains how shareholder value should enter all of our corporate decisions.

"In the current environment, the goal must be to earn a return above the cost of capital. If you can do that, you're building a strong company, one that can take advantage of business opportunities as they arise.

"Now, the improved returns can go to the shareholders directly through higher dividends or other payouts of capital which will prompt a lot of politically motivated handwringing. Or you can take that capital and put it to work in projects where you expect to do well in the future. But that's where serious problems can arise. The corporate urge to waste capital by reinvesting in shrinking industries, or maybe even worse, by diversifying out of them, is hard to resist. That's why attention to share values as a reliable means of gauging the value of various possibilities is so important. Shareholder value should be the yardstick."

With all of the above information as guidance to our deliberations, we evaluated a series of companies, mainly in the electronics systems areas, to determine if any of them would make good strategic partners. Our financial position was improved but we still had to be cautious that we took care not to engage in any out-of-control auction that would reverse the progress that we had already made.

Our First Serious Look at an Acquisition

As we began looking seriously at companies with which we could partner, it became obvious to us that industry consolidations throughout the country were already off to a fast start. IBM, who we all had grown up knowing as a pillar of industry, was having problems. They had built their reputation with huge, main-frame computers. Things in the computer world were moving at a rapid pace with technology changes guiding the way. The personal computer industry was going through its period of crazy expansion and IBM suddenly found itself in serious financial trouble.

When Louis Gerstner took over the company in 1992 IBM posted a loss of $5 billion that year. The previous year they had sold their typewriter business but in 1992 they slashed their dividend and planned to drop their work force by 50,000 people. For the first nine months of that year IBM had posted a deficit of $8.4 billion after taking into consideration restructuring charges. Federal Systems that year was IBM's only bright spot with earnings of $71 million on sales of $2.2 billion. Gerstner decided to sell the Federal Systems business and use the money to help finance a complete restructuring of the company.

Federal Systems has a fairly diverse stable of products and services including some significant work in systems integration. A major contract they had won from the FAA involved design of a completely new air traffic control system. That project was in a serious overrun condition.

Grumman decided to take a serious look at Federal Systems. There was a good deal of synergy with Grumman's core business, but some of management wasn't convinced that it was the type of purchase that would give us any improved technical capability or open up any new market segments. There was also concern among some that the Data Systems Group might not have the management capability to handle the integration of Federal Systems.

We knew that there were several other companies interested in acquiring Federal Systems and we knew that might drive the bidding too high to satisfy our appetite. We did some serious analysis and valued the company at about $800 million. Bob Anderson, Grumman's Chief Financial Officer believed that number was much too high for Grumman and we decided not to submit a bid. The winning bid was submitted by the Loral Corporation for $1.58 billion.

We had only recently begun to look at Loral as a possible partner but we soon put that possibility aside. At that time Loral was on a tear to acquire other companies.

In the 1970's Loral was in terrible financial shape. In 1971 it had lost $3 million and was unable to make its loan payments.

In 1972 Loral was on the verge of bankruptcy when it was purchased by Bernard Schwartz. Over the course of the next couple of decades Schwartz built the company into a major player in the aerospace and defense business. The company was built by acquisitions. Schwartz believed that with the need for new weapon systems diminishing, there would be a growing demand for upgrading of existing systems and he was concentrating his efforts on building capability on that direction. He had previously purchased LTV Missile Division for $261 million, Ford Aerospace Corp for $715 million, Fairchild Weston for $185 million, Goodyear Aerospace for $640 million and it goes on and on. Obviously it was futile at the time to consider Loral as a candidate for partnering.

Retrospective

Bernie Swartz made a series of acquisitions that built Loral into a major player in the aerospace industry and solidified his reputation as one of the serious entrepreneurs in the US. In 1996 he sold Loral to Lockheed Martin for nearly $10 billion. Lockheed paid around $7 billion in stock and took on more than $3 billion in debt through this transaction. When the company was folded into Lockheed Martin it was split in two. Lockheed absorbed the military electronics business and split off a company called Loral Space and Communications Corporation. Was Swartz finished with his company? No, he was appointed the leader of this new company and immediately indicated he already had a few acquisitions in mind to start building a new empire.

Adjusting To the New Strategy

As soon as Grumman's new strategic statement was published in September of 1993, we began to turn the wheels internally to adjust not only our operating mentality, but our entire management structure. Creating or improving shareholder value meant that all operating managers needed to start thinking differently. Creating shareholder value means earning returns that are greater than the company's cost of capital. This meant that each operating unit was expected to implement a results oriented program of asset reduction, operating profit improvement and where possible, business realignments. This activity was designated the company's Performance Improvement Program (PIP) described earlier.

Management clearly stated that businesses that did not create value would be re-evaluated to achieve needed improvements or be scheduled for sale or phase-out in order to free up funds for investment in value creating businesses. The intent was to increase Grumman's plummeting credit rating to a stable "A" rating.

The hope was that Grumman's mature businesses would improve their positive cash flow, permitting these funds to be used for other value creating opportunities, pay down debt or return the funds to the shareholders if the funds could not be otherwise used to create shareholder value.

For the period from 1986 through 1990, Grumman's working capital experience as a percentage of sales was nearly twice that of both the competition's aircraft or electronics segments. By 1992 aggressive internal programs had brought that working capital ratio down to about 10% higher than our competitors.

From 1986 through 1990, Grumman's earnings (before interest and taxes) were about equal to our aircraft competitors but nearly half our electronics competitors. In 1991 we began to improve those earnings but we were still significantly below the competitor averages.

A restructuring team was established in 1993 and prepared a comprehensive implementation plan to be implemented in 1994 that would consolidate all aircraft manufacturing and modification programs, technical and program operations, laboratory and prototype operations and computer operations.

Detailed parts and machining operations were to be outsourced, current facilities reduced by 30%, staff reductions would amount to 2000 people, manufacturing labor rates were to be reduced by 50% with an accompanying reduction in production costs of about 16%.

As a result of these planned activities a restructuring charge of $58.1 million related to fixed asset write-offs was taken in 1993. It was believed that if all of the planned changes could be rapidly implemented, Grumman would be in a better position to participate in the acquisition game. But time was getting critical.

We had learned from our earlier attempt to participate in the IBM Federal Systems sale, that there were several companies out there that were already in a position to be acquisition aggressive and although our Performance Improvement Plan was aggressive, time was our enemy.

Were We Caught Off Guard?

The question has often been asked "why did all of this happen so fast, did we get caught off guard?" To provide a simple answer requires some knowledge of how the Government procurement system works. Grumman was not totally dependent on the F-14 for its annual revenue. The company had built up its arsenal of products over the years but the F-14 was certainly a large part of our future business projections. I can still remember when we were working on the original F-14 proposal in the 1960's. Lew Evans, who was president at the time wanted every employee to understand how important it was for Grumman to win this competition. During the weeks of proposal preparation, Evans had signs placed in very visible spots of every plant reading **"the F-14 is like life—consider the alternative"**. The events that followed are a reminder of just how correct these words were.

As important as the program was to our business base, the truth was that the F-14 represented Grumman's continued presence as a major tactical aircraft prime contractor. The F-14 program kept Grumman in the same category as McDonnell Douglas, General Dynamics, Lockheed and Northrop as builders of significant military aircraft. With no F-14's in our production arsenal, it was unlikely that Grumman could remain in the "prime contractor" arena. Lew Evans knew that-hence his signs.

The first flight of the F-14 took place in December of 1970 with the final development aircraft being flown in 1971. The first Tomcats off the Calverton production line were sent to the Navy in October of 1972. The original pentagon requirement for the F-14 was to have the capability to take on six different targets at the same time. In November of 1973 at the Naval Missile Test Center at Point Mugu, California, six AIM-54 missiles were fired from an F-14, at six target drones simultaneously. Five of the six hit their designated targets with one missing. The one miss was caused by a missile malfunction, not any error of the F-14 system. At that point the Pentagon was sold on the aircraft.

Over the years there were several improvements in the engines and the systems of the F-14. The new F-14D was put into production in 1988. Plans at that time called for the delivery of 127 new production F-14D's and the modification of 400 F-14A's to the D configuration.

In 1989 the Navy (or someone) decided to phase out the F-14 reconnaissance mission and assign it to the F-18 Hornets. During Operation desert Storm however, the F-14 flew 781 reconnaissance missions.

Much to everyones surprise, the revised defense budget submitted in April of 1989 proposed cancelling all new production of the aircraft. Due largely to Grumman's full court press in Washington, congress did authorize 18 new F-14D's for 1990 with the stipulation that these would be the last new aircraft authorized, a total of 37, not the originally planned 127 aircraft. The first F-14D was delivered in February of 1990.

This seems to be the point in history where sensible politics fell victim to high level political brinkmanship. Because of a fever-like mood in Washington to make big cuts in the defense budget, all F-14 production money for 1991 was eliminated and no money was authorized for 1992 and 1993. The final blow was delivered in February of 1991 when the Navy cancelled the already funded $780 million contract for the 12 re-manufactured F-14's, effectively ending the program.

Grumman had watched all of these events carefully and we participated in deliberations wherever we could. Our Washington office was working in high gear for months during the deliberations trying to make our case for the F-14. We visited nearly every congressman who had influence on the defense budget deliberations, especially those who had some of our sub-contractors located in their districts. Our argument, for those who would listen, was that the money for the development of the F-14D had already been spent and that aircraft had far more capability than an upgraded F-18. The F-18 as it existed would need a complete re-design to accommodate the performance capability of the F-14D. The F-18E would be a single seat version with the F-18F being a two seat version. These are very significant modifications, essentially creating a new aircraft. The engines would be new and more powerful than those on the current F-18, the wings needed a complete re-design making them larger and utilizing composite material. The landing gear needed to be made stronger. In effect this was to be nearly a complete new airplane design. When all of this was completed, the new f-18 would barely have the capability of the F-14D which was already flying with all of its capability already paid for. The facts were so clear that we felt that even a member of congress should be able to understand it.

The Long Island congressional delegation pledged to help us but their weak positioning on important committees that influenced defense spending was of little help. They did manage to have a meeting with then Secretary of Defense Dick Cheney, but they felt from that meeting that the die had been cast. Cheney had been convinced that he could save $2.4 billion over a five year period. The argument that development money which had already been spent on the now flying F-14D was going to be spent all over again on the F-18 re-design, fell on deaf ears.

The only fallback that Grumman had at this point was to make a legal argument that the F-18 D and E were essentially new aircraft and a program of that magnitude should be sent out for re-bid as a new program. It was pretty clear to Grumman management that even if we were to win that argument, any new award would almost certainly go to McDonnell Douglas. We would have spent a pile of money on a proposal, and made many more enemies in Washington only to have the same decision made.

As I think back to John O'Brien's motivation to put Grumman in a better geo-political environment, the F-14 story is a great testimonial to his strategy.

Without a doubt, those members of the Grumman management team who worked the Washington scene for many years, believed, the key Navy brass wanted the F-14 over the F-18. Early in 1990, an edition of Long Island's Newsday was headlined that the Navy's choice was the F-14, and the F-18 would be procured for one more year and then the line would be shut down. Whatever Newsday's source, (probably a Navy source) this was great news for Grumman and exactly what our intelligence had indicated.

Apparently whoever in Washington released that announcement did not clear it far enough up the decision chain-of-command. In short order and despite our best efforts, that decision was reversed. If one stands back far enough to see all of the events that took place, one would have to consider that the decision was purely political and had little to do with Navy's wants or needs.

Who Really Calls The Shots?

In a free enterprise system, most would think that public companies are in control of their own destiny. For the most part that is true except for companies that do business with the Government, specifically the Department Of Defense. When President Reagan ended the Cold War, Grumman, like every other large company knew that the defense budget would eventually decline in value, hence the beginning of our studies to re-plot our future. Traditionally these changes came slowly because most large defense programs were based upon long term production contracts like the F-14. When President Bush took over with Dick Cheney as his Defense Secretary, these program reviews were accelerated. Because program cuts meant job cuts, congress was very involved in every one of these program decisions.

When President Clinton was running for President in 1992, he used Congressman Les Aspin as his advisor on defense issues. Aspin was the Chairman of the House Armed Services Committee at the time and was familiar with defense issues. When Bill Clinton was elected, he appointed Aspin as his Secretary of Defense. Almost from the first day in his new position, Secretary Aspin was at odds with Pentagon leaders and military brass.

The Defense Industry was initially happy about Aspin's appointment, assuming that he would continue his position of favoring a strong military industrial base. But that changed quickly. Aspin now favored large cutbacks in the size of the military and found himself in serious disagreement with General Colin Powell, then chairman of the Joint Chiefs of Staff.

Secretary Aspin launched a "bottoms up review" of the US Defense posture which concluded that the entire defense industry needed to be restructured. Aspin called a meeting of the major defense industry leaders to brief them on his findings. Aspin opened the meeting but quickly turned it over to his Deputy Defense Secretary, William Perry. This meeting, which has been referred to as "The Last Supper," boldly informed these industry leaders that the industry was going to have to shrink by more than 40 percent to remain in balance with declining post-Cold War defense budgets. It followed that it was necessary to reduce the assets allocated to defense in both private and public sectors. In simpler terms this meant that when all of the reductions were over, only about half of the large defense companies would survive.

The Department Of Defense intended to similarly reduce its asset base by closing government owned facilities, bases and shipyards, depots and laboratories. The theory was that to accomplish these actions new policies were necessary to permit the downsized companies to share in the cost savings that resulted from their actions.

Congress had other ideas. Congressional reaction to these initiatives was negative as would be expected. Downsizing meant fewer jobs in congressional districts. Even though Congress generally agreed that industry and government downsizing was necessary it took on the "not in my district" attitude as had been congressional policy for many years. Congress termed the DoD defense industry policy "payoffs for layoffs" and they placed severe limitations on government sharing of savings with private industry. This was very typical of how the political system worked and still works today. The attitude of Congress seems to be to kill any creative ideas but never come up with a better solution.

Secretary Aspin became controversial on almost every front to the point where he was an embarrassment to President Clinton. With little leadership accomplishment to his record, Aspin resigned after serving one year in office and was replaced by William Perry who was the Deputy Secretary. During Perry's reign as Defense Secretary, massive consolidation of the defense industry took place.

It should be easy for all of us to imagine the turmoil that was taking place in Washington during this part of the 1990's. Every elected official was acting on behalf of their constituents to insure that the "hurt" was spread elsewhere. Should anyone be surprised that Grumman's political weakness played a big part in decisions that eventually effected the company's survival?

This is a good point to introduce another short story. Long after the decision was announced to cancel the F-14D and go with the F-18E/F, Grumman CEO Renso Caporali was asked to give a presentation on the design of the F-14 to an AIAA group at The University of Buffalo. The following are Chairman Caporali's words:

"After the presentation, an Air Force Colonel who was in attendance asked me why the F-18 was chosen over the F-14. I replied that the reason given by then Secretary of Defense Cheney was cost. This would have been a valid reason had the two programs been at the same point in their evolution. However at that point in time the advanced F-14 development dollars had already been spent, with the design and development successfully completed while the F-18 E/F costs had yet to even be estimated. Clearly acquisition cost was not a valid reason.

"The questioner indicated that he agreed with me, then quite logically asked, "but why them?" My reply was that to be fair we have to realize that McDonnell Douglas was the nation's largest aerospace-defense entity and involved in more programs of importance to the defense of the nation than Grumman. That might therefore have been a valid reason for wanting to keep it healthy if a choice between the two companies had to be made. I added that it might be worth noting that the presidential election year of 1992 was close at hand at which time the then-current administration of George H.W.Bush would be running for their second term.

The State of New York, home of Grumman and the plants that produced the F-14D was undoubtedly expected to go for the Democratic opposition. Inasmuch as that is the case that presidential candidates rarely set foot in the state except to attend fund raising events, generally held in new York city. On the other hand, Missouri is frequently considered a swing state and that is where McDonnell Douglas was headquartered and the F-18 is assembled. I further added that at that time the Democratic Governor of New York was Mario Cuomo who was thought by many to be a possible Democratic Party candidate for President. Just maybe all of this might have had a bearing on the outcome of the F-14/F-18 saga."

As events evolved, Gov. Cuomo did not run and democrat Bill Clinton was elected. With the change in administration the speed of disarmament ratcheted up a notch and the need to find a way to survive, much less prosper, became even more intense."

Retrospective

With the decision on the F-18 over the F-14 having been made by the Secretary of Defense, the Navy was handed the task of justifying the choice based on cost. The Navy saluted and set about doing the job. Eventually the Navy announced that the F-18 was more economical if purchased in quantities of 1000 or greater. This would keep the airplane operational through the 2020's. Ten years later in 2012 the Navy stated that the next budget request would call for a buy of 500 aircraft. The Navy indicated that it had not intended to even go for this buy except that the delays in the Lockheed F-35C had forced it to change plans. It would appear that the cost advantage of the F-18 over the F-14 was short of being realized. Surprise! Surprise!

By this time Grumman was making significant strides to improve its financial position to the point where it was possible to consider growth by some small acquisitions.

A Quick Look at LTV

Most long term Grummanites are familiar with the events of the 1980's when in 1981 the LTV Corporation made a move to purchase 70% of the stock of Grumman. The details of that attempt are well documented. The final result of that takeover attempt was that the purchase was blocked on antitrust grounds. This, of course, is a simple way of describing a very volatile period at Grumman. It was the first real threat to Grumman's independence. Because of the internal campaign at Grumman, a significant amount of company stock was eventually held by its employees, who rallied in the attempt to beat off the takeover attempt. This was also a true view into the loyalty Grumman's employees had for their Company.

As a result of re-organizations and management changes at LTV, that company was re-named LTV Aerospace and Defense Company in April of 1983. The company was re-organized into two divisions, the Missiles and Advance Programs Division and the Aero Products Division. In 1986 these divisions were again renamed the Missiles and Electronics Group and the Aircraft Products Group.

Poor business results in LTV's steel and energy businesses forced the company to enter a long and litigious bankruptcy in July of 1986. LTV Aerospace and Defense Co. was consistently profitable with sales of $2.3 billion in 1985 and earnings that year of $164 million. LTV was placing its hopes at that time on the YA-7F, an upgrade of the A-4 Corsair II attack jet. This program was the company's last big program as a prime contractor (does this sound familiar?) The Air Force, however, had different ideas. The service preferred the General Dynamics F-16.

This was a death blow to LTV who had sales in 1989 of $700 million. As might be expected, the Aerospace and Defense Division began a period of intense re-organization and re-planning. It was about this time that I was invited to

Dallas by Gordon Williams, President of LTV's Aerospace and Defense Division to interview for a job in the division's re-organized headquarters. When I arrived for the interview, the management was in a panic mode to put out some unexpected fires in their business plan. The interview was horrific and I left Dallas with a bad taste in my mouth. Days after I returned to Long Island, Gordon Williams called me to apologize for the state of affairs at the time of my arrival and asked me to meet with him the next week when he was planning to be in New York City on business. I agreed and we met and had a business-like chat about the possibility of me joining his management team. In the interim I had done a little more research on the condition of the company and decided not to make the move.

In May of 1991, the LTV bankruptcy resulted in the Aerospace and Defense Division being offered for sale. The Irony of this situation begins here. Grumman was still in the throws of the budget battles on both the A-6 and F-14 programs. Renso Caporali was astute enough to visualize some of the handwriting on the wall as to what might be Grumman's fate, if the budget pendulum swung the wrong way. Caporali asked me to take a small team to Dallas to evaluate LTV as a possible acquisition. I formed a team from Accounting, Business Development, and Manufacturing and off to Dallas we went. This was intended to be a very preliminary look at the company. If we found cause to look further, we would send a more comprehensive team to perform a due diligence analysis.

When we arrived at LTV, the scene was somewhat embarrassing. Who greeted us but Gordon Williams, the same person that had offered me a job only weeks earlier. He shook my hand, leaned over slightly and said, "strange turn of events". The Grumman team spent two days at the LTV facility. Perhaps the most interesting part of our visit was a tour we got of their "Hummer" facility. LTV had become the manufacturer of the Hummer and it was perhaps one of the more interesting things they had to show us, but certainly not within the area of business Grumman had any interest in. We returned home with a report indicating that Grumman had no real synergy with this company.

Soon after our return, Martin Marietta and Lockheed put together a bid of $355 million for the unit. Another bid was made by Thompson SA, a French aerospace giant. Their bid raised some political questions regarding foreign ownership in the US defense industry. The final successful bidder was Northrop partnered with The Carlyle Group. They purchased what was called the Vought Aircraft Group for $230 million, while Loral paid $244 million for the Missiles and Space Division, renaming it Loral Vought Systems.

Next Was Chrysler Technologies Corp

The Electronics Systems segment of Grumman came forward with an analysis that suggested we consider the possible acquisition of Chrysler Technologies Corp. That company employed about 4000 people at the time, mostly in Alabama and Texas. They were involved in aircraft modifications, electronics, and communications. We had estimated the value of that company at about $200 million, which was right in the ball park of what we could afford for an acquisition. Their sales at that time were around $400 million annually and they appeared to be a good fit with our new strategic direction. Unfortunately, we got in on the evaluation late in the process where others had already made thorough evaluations and were in the process of making offers. We simply didn't move fast enough and Raytheon moved in with a quick acquisition.

A Serious Look at E Systems

Chairman Caporali didn't need any more studies to tell him that things were moving fast within the aerospace industry. More alarming than the pace of acquisitions were the prices that were being bid in takeovers. It was obvious that Grumman was not in a position financially to seriously participate in the acquisition game. The best route was through some form of partnership or merger.

We had carefully studied several electronics companies and one that stood out having good synergy with Grumman was E Systems. In addition to a good fit of technology and products, E Systems had a large portfolio of programs in what was then known as the "dark world." Grumman had also built up a fairly good stable of programs in that market.

E Systems at that time was one of the leading companies in defense electronics. They had a diversified series of products covering surveillance, verification, and aircraft ground-land navigation equipment. Their customer base was international but much of their business fell into the categories of national security, being split between intelligence and reconnaissance command, control and communications.

The history of the company is interesting. It was created in 1964 when LTV Temco Aerospace Division of Ling-Temco-Vought Inc. formed LTV Electrosystems. The following year LTV Electrosystems became a public subsidiary and was listed on the over-the-counter market. During that year it acquired all of the properties of its parent company. In 1965 the company sales were $81 million.

From 1965 to 1972 the company concentrated on expansion through a series of acquisitions. By 1970 sales had grown to over $200 million. In 1972 the company was re-named E Systems. By the middle of the 1970's E Systems was the world's top supplier of military radios and large earth station antennas for satellite communications. At this point their sales were about 55% defense contracts and 45% international and non-defense.

By 1983 their sales had grown to over $827 million and they had booked sales of another $900 million. For the first time in its history E Systems had sales in 1986 that exceeded $1 billion with an employment level of more than 15,000. At this point they began a series of acquisitions.

In 1992 as the cold war ended a major contract with the German government was cancelled resulting in the loss of potential work amounting to nearly $1 billion.

The timing seemed right for considering some form of partnership or a new business arrangement for E Systems. Our analysis showed that there was a great deal of synergy with the products of both companies. We were both active in electronic warfare, aircraft modifications, electronics and data fusion, data systems, and technical services. The market capitalization of both companies was nearly identical at around $1.4 billion. Their operating margins were greater than Grumman's, but financially we were almost a 50/50 fit. In terms of shareholder value added, this combination seemed like a no brainer.

Any merger with E systems, by itself, would not be the end game, but it would put the combined company in a better position to look at still further acquisitions in the future. Perhaps as importantly, a merger of this type would send a strong signal of the direction Grumman had chosen to take, possibly abandoning it's prime aircraft role to build itself as the electronics system integrator of choice for future programs.

At this early point in our studies and deliberations, we had not yet made the final decision to move in this direction, but we were aware that nearly every other defense company was making the same evaluations. Waiting might not be in our best interest.

We made arrangements for Renso Caporali to meet with the chairman of E Systems for an informal talk about the industry's future. Cappy and I flew to Dallas for the meeting and he met with the CEO to determine if there was any interest on their part in getting together.

As I recall it, at that time, the top management of E Systems was in a temporary state of affairs. The CEO was ill and the company was being run by a temporary CEO. The discussion was a one- on-one: I remained outside the office as did their executive staff. After discussing the state of the current government business arena, Caporali asked if there might be room for further discussions of a possible combination of our two companies. The answer that he got was a little surprising. The E Systems CEO indicated that they had no interest in any merger with anyone at that time. He also indicated that government money was pouring in and he saw no immediate need to consider any type of partnership. He further indicated that if Grumman was willing to make an offer to acquire the company, E Systems would have to consider it. As I stated previously, an acquisition at that time was not in our planning process, especially one that would not improve our position as a weapon systems prime contractor.

Retrospective

Our visit to E Systems was in mid 1993. Later in 1993 when East and West Germany became unified, Germany announced a freeze on defense contracts. Since E Systems had major contracts with the Germans on the EGRETT aircraft program, this cancellation put a serious strain on E Systems profits. In 1995 E Systems entered into an agreement to merge with the Raytheon Company. Raytheon planned to take their RTN Acquisition Corporation, a wholly owned subsidiary of

Raytheon and merge it with E Systems and make E Systems a wholly owned subsidiary of Raytheon.

Was A Merger The Right Move?

The trend for the business community to move in the direction of mergers and acquisitions has been characterized as a series of acquisition waves that have taken place since the first merger wave in the 1890's. There have been five distinct merger waves since then

The first merger wave took place as a result of the economic depression that existed at that time. Most of these mergers were directed at reducing product prices to increase corporate sales and assist in corporate survival. When the equity market crashed in 1903-05, this merger wave came to an abrupt end.

The second wave took place around 1910. The First World War kept merger activity at a minimum until around this time. New anti-trust laws were put into place that started the second wave of mergers that lasted until about 1929 when the stock market crashed and sent us into a world-wide depression.

The Second World War held off the next merger wave. After the end of the war, the third merger wave started in the 1950's, peaked in 1968 and collapsed in 1973 when the oil crisis again pushed us into another world recession. Tightening the anti-trust laws in the early 1950's caused US companies to move toward diversification. These new laws encouraged companies to look at diversification by acquiring companies outside their own industries. In the 1960's, companies were looking toward forming conglomerate organizations. This was the era of the conglomerate company. It sounded good on paper but it was later proven to be a faulty concept.

The fourth wave of mergers started in 1981 when the stock market recovered from the previous recession. This was the period when corporate managers realized that the earlier move to conglomerates was unsuccessful. This period was defined by divestitures of many of the pieces of companies that simply did not fit their business strategy. This move triggered still more changes in the anti-trust laws, de-regulation of the financial services sector and creation of the "junk bond market." The period was defined by large divestitures, hostile takeovers, leveraged buy-outs (LBO'S) and management buy-outs (MBO'S). This period required managers to completely de-emphasize the conglomerate mentality and focus on the company's core business. Companies that didn't react to the need to re-focus became targets of hostile raiders who were ready to do the restructuring for them. Conglomerate structures were deemed ineffective and had no ability to react to industry shocks. The 1980's saw the emergence of hostile takeovers by corporate raiders like Carl Icahn and T. Boone Pickens. These men became household names.

The fifth wave of mergers started in 1990 and ran through 2003. During this period there were more than 100,000 mergers and acquisitions in the United States contrasted to the 30,000 that were accomplished in the fourth merger wave period. This fifth wave was responding to shrinking markets and projections of smaller business bases in nearly every market segment. Emphasis in the 1990's merger activities were aimed at improvements in shareholder value. That is exactly where Grumman was positioned at the time.

The Need For Secrecy

As early as that first executive meeting in 1991, Chairman Caporali continued to express the need for a very high level of confidentiality in the studies that were being conducted to map Grumman's future. We carefully selected each employee that participated in the study work and tried to compartmentalize lower level studies so as not to give any hint of what the eventual goal of the studies was. For the early studies, secrecy was less important because we were only trying to determine the alternative actions that would keep Grumman whole, either in the prime aircraft market or in the electronics and data markets. In the later stages of the studies however, as it appeared more and more like some form of combination with another company would likely be necessary, secrecy was a prime concern.

Perhaps this drive for silence was created by the fact that all of us on Grumman's management team had been trained in the 1970's and 1980's when corporate raiders were constantly on the prowl for under-valued companies. During just one year, 1988, there were nearly 4000 takeovers by corporate raiders.

Even in the 1990's, when defense companies were planning for the announced reductions in military spending, it was important not to give any hint that a company was open for a possible acquisition. Information of this type, especially for a company that was considered to be under-valued as Grumman was, it was considered dangerous to send any signal of an interest in partnering with another company.

It was also very important to understand the not-so-subtle differences in the various techniques that were available for companies to become partners. We had already made the decision that Grumman was not in a financial position to make a significant acquisition of another company. The most attractive arrangement would be a friendly merger with a company of similar size and capability. To better understand this concept, it might be helpful to discuss the differences between mergers and acquisitions (takeovers).

In the broadest sense, a merger and a takeover are very similar in their results. They combine two formerly independent companies into a new single legal organization. Regardless of which form of combination is accomplished, there is always a common goal of improved company performance and better shareholder value over a long period. These gains usually take the form of significant increases in sales, economies of scale from a larger company, greater share of a specific market creating a better competitive position, broadened diversification, and sometimes tax efficiencies. However, the business rationale and financing methods between mergers and takeovers are very different.

Grumman's primary motivation was to protect, as much as possible, its core capabilities and to do that through retention of most of its employees and its key facilities. We also had a long standing pride in the Grumman name and wanted that protected. The culture of the company was a large part of our past successes and it was important to partner with a company that had a similar culture if possible. To accomplish these goals, the only avenue that appeared possible was to avoid acquisition and work toward a merger.

A merger implies a friendly mutual decision by two companies to combine into a new single company. It is generally considered to be a decision made by two companies of relatively equal size and capability. The theory of a merger of equals is to put two companies together as a single legal entity that is worth more than the sum of the individual parts. In a merger, shares of one company are normally exchanged for an equal value of shares in the new company.

As perfect as this all sounds, the efficiencies of scale do not come free of pain. When the two companies are combined, the gains in value to both groups of shareholders comes from structural and organizational consolidations that cut costs and improve profits resulting in increased shareholder value. The advantage of a merger however, is that changes are normally relatively slow and the managements of both parties have a say in all consolidation actions.

A takeover on the other hand is normally the purchase of one company by another company, usually a bigger one. This results in the combination of "un-equals" and will produce the same advantages as a merger, but without the benefit of mutual decision making. Changes in a takeover are normally faster in order to achieve financial gains as fast as possible to help pay for the cost of the acquisition. Unlike a merger, the acquiring company pays cash for the stock of the acquired company. Stock conversions can also be a form of payment but either way the purchasing company essentially finances the purchase of the target company, buying it outright for the shareholders. The obvious business strategy in a takeover is to make changes that produce financial gains as soon as possible after the takeover. In a takeover situation, the management of the acquired company usually has little or no influence on future events. In most cases the top management of the acquired company is replaced soon after the takeover, unless some other agreement accompanied the acquisition.

It should be obvious, that a merger was the desired path for Grumman. Past history has shown that activities leading to a friendly merger, which often take weeks or even months, sometimes find their way into the public domain creating a condition where some company other than the desired partner, hears of the discussions and decides it will make a hostile takeover move, hence the need for strict secrecy in all merger discussions.

When merger discussions move beyond the initial discussion phase and it appears that some form of combination is going to take place, a firm is usually brought in to guide the merger process. When our studies started to show that a merger would be Grumman's best path, we enlisted the services of Goldman Sachs to insure that all of the correct evaluations were made and that all required legal avenues were covered during deliberations.

Since our Project X team was looking at selecting the best merger partner for Grumman, one aspect of any potential merger was the relative strength of Grumman in the partnership compared to the selected partner. Goldman Sachs had done some fairly complete evaluations, based on the latest available financial data, for each of the companies that we were seriously considering. One method that we used to determine the friendliness of a combination was to look at the market capitalization ratios of each of the companies being considered. These ratios would provide some forward look at just how equal each partner would be considered in a merger of equals.

By examining the capitalization ratios of each potential merger partner, it would tell us just how much power Grumman would have in final merger decisions. In other words if two companies combine, the company that brings the greater financial power to the merger will likely have the greater say. An ideal merger of equals would be two companies that had equal financial power and a 50% share of the capitalization ratio. The list that follows, based on Goldman Sachs evaluations, shows the ratios for all of the companies that we seriously considered in our deliberations.

Capitalization Ratio of Potential Partners	
Company	Ratio
E Systems	50%
Grumman	50%
Northrop	57%
Grumman	43%
Loral	69%
Grumman	31%
Lockheed	74.9%
Grumman	25.1%
Martin Marietta	75.1%
Grumman	24.9%
McDonnell Douglas	75.3%
Grumman	24.7%
Raytheon	86.2%
Grumman	13.8%
GM Hughes	92%
Grumman	8%

Based on this method of classifying possible partners, E Systems was the most attractive partner with Hughes taking up the bottom position. We did make a serious attempt to discuss a merger with E Systems. Boeing was not listed in the above chart because it was not possible at the time for Goldman Sachs to separate the market cap for their defense segment. Bill Perry, our consultant with these studies felt strongly that Boeing should be our first target for a merger.

Boeing had been a huge military supplier during the Second World War but they were now concentrating on commercial aircraft business. They had made several ventures into military work but they had bad experiences on most of them. Boeing was concerned by what they called the "boom or bust" business cycles in the commercial aircraft business. They, like we, knew that the business cycles for commercial aircraft and the cycle for military aircraft seemed to be almost exactly 180 degrees out of phase. This suggested that a properly run company that had balanced business in both arenas could perform very well in terms of a stable business base and solid profits.

The time seemed right. Our thought was to suggest that a merger of the two companies would provide Boeing with a strong defense related partner that knew how to do business in that arena. Grumman could concentrate exclusively on the defense business leaving the current Boeing management to direct their attention at continuing profitability with commercial aircraft. Frank Shrontz was Boeing's CEO at that time. Renso Caporali arranged a meeting with Shrontz, proposing further discussion possibly leading to a merger of the two companies. The discussions were not negative but they were also not positive. Shrontz indicated that Boeing's past performance on some military programs left a bad taste in their mouths. He also indicated that management was under pressure from the Board to insure a successful development of the new 777 aircraft. It was highly unlikely that the Board of Directors would look favorably on any moves that might take management attention away from that goal. But, Shrontz indicated that he would have Boeing management take it under consideration as a possible future move.

Returning from that discussion, Caporali sat with Bill Perry, our consultant, to discuss the situation with Boeing. Perry agreed that Boeing was probably the best fit for Grumman in terms of keeping the company intact. It was also a move that would probably be considered the end game to keep the new company prominent as a prime contractor for military aircraft. But Perry did not think that Grumman could wait for Boeing to get to the point of a decision, especially if that decision was delayed until the 777 development was successfully completed. Perry suggested that Grumman continue to look at other options.

There had been some whispered rumors among some of Grumman's management about an attempt Boeing had made years earlier to discuss a possible merger. Boeing had been losing money on many of the military programs that it had been awarded. The story goes that the Chairman of Boeing visited Jack Bierwirth, suggesting that with Grumman's success record on military programs over the years, it might be advantageous to both companies if we looked at the possibility of getting together in some manner. Bierwirth supposedly turned Boeing away, flatly refusing to have any discussions on the subject. Is it possible that this meeting actually happened and the Boeing executives were reacting to that event? We will never know. However, less than a year after refusing Caporali's merger suggestion, Boeing took the initiative to merge with McDonnell Douglas, a company that had a history quite similar to Grumman's.

The two remaining Aircraft companies that we evaluated were McDonnell Douglas and Lockheed. Our consensus was that any partnership with Lockheed would likely result in Grumman being completely absorbed by Lockheed. There were not the synergy advantages that would result in a company being anything but one large company with the same basic capabilities as each of the individual companies. There would be no real added value resulting from such a merger. The capitalization ratio with Lockheed would also seem to place Grumman at a serious negative position in terms of relative company power in a merger.

With the exception of the capitalization ratio factor, McDonnell Douglas also seemed to be a good candidate. Both Grumman and McDonnell Douglas had similar product lines and basically the same technology capabilities. The problem, however, was that there seemed to be significant cultural differences in the two companies. The fact that Grumman and McDonnell had been fierce competitors ever since the formation of both companies gave rise to the opinion that the employees of neither company would ever accept any combination. The cultural concern by itself was not enough to keep us from seriously considering a partnership with McDonnell. The real issue was the belief that even if we were able to get together, the Government would most likely stop the merger based on a strong objection by the Navy.

The next step was to consider Northrop. A year earlier Northrop's CEO Kent Kresa had met with CEO Caporali in New York. At that time Kresa seemed less than enthused about getting together. Caporali once again called Kresa and indicated that we were considering all of our alternatives and he would like to have our study team meet with Northrop's business strategy people to openly discuss future possibilities. Kresa agreed that a preliminary meeting would be fine with no commitments made.

We had evaluated Northrop as we did all other major defense players. Northrop looked good in terms of the synergy matches and there was definitely that 2+2=5 possibility. The capitalization ratios of the two companies were favorable to a merger of equals. We felt that Grumman's electronics integration capability would be a strong addition to the Northrop capabilities. In addition Grumman had been doing a good deal of technological research into programs that might offer strong future possibilities for entering new related product lines. Initially the only concern we had about Northrop was that a merger would not be the end game. Together we would still not be a guaranteed defense industry survivor. More acquisitions or mergers would be necessary to put the combined company in a lead position as one of at least the top three defense companies. With all of this in mind I scheduled a meeting with my counterpart at Northrop, Jim Roche. My team consisted of Bob Denien, Dick Anderson and me. I divided the presentation into three parts, giving the overview and business presentation myself, allowing Bob Denien to discuss our aircraft related programs and Dick Anderson discussing all of our other technology capabilities. It was not our plan at this initial meeting to discuss mergers or acquisitions but simply to present Grumman as we were. Northrop had been primarily an Air Force company and they were not too familiar with Grumman.

Jim Roche was a dominating figure. His job at Northrop was essentially the same as mine at Grumman except that in addition to corporate strategy and technology, Roche also controlled Northrop's Public Affairs group. Roche had served in the Navy and risen to the rank of Captain. During his Navy career his assignments included Principal Deputy Director of the State Department's Policy Plannng Staff. He was also assigned as Senior Professional Staff Member of the Senate Select Committee on Intelligence. Further Roche also served as Staff Director to the Senate Armed Services Committee under the chairmanship of Senator Sam Nunn of Georgia, who was the powerful chairman of that committee. Roche came across as a very intelligent individual, very pleasant yet a very dominating one. He and his team listened to our presentation, we had lunch and without any plans scheduled for more meetings we got back on our Gulfstream and returned to New York.

About a week later I received a call from Roche indicating that Northrop would like to have further discussions, providing Grumman with a similar presentation of their company capabilities. Roche suggested that we schedule a three day visit to their headquarters in Los Angeles so that they could give us a quick tour of some of their facilities and also to discuss synergies between the two companies. With that type of invitation, I knew that this was more than just a courtesy meeting, Northrop had more than a passing interest in Grumman.

Bob Denien, Dick Anderson, and I scheduled the company's Gulfstream for another trip to Los Angeles. The beauty of using Grumman's Gulfstream was two-fold. We could use the four hour trip to seriously discuss our meeting strategy, but as importantly, all of our discussions would be in the strictest privacy of our own aircraft. For this second visit we decided that we would concentrate on getting a complete understanding of Northrop's technical and manufacturing capabilities as well as the company culture and business practices. Northrop had dealt primarily with the Air Force. Grumman and Northrop had rarely gone head to head as competitors. We would look for synergies between the two companies with emphasis on improving competitiveness for future programs. We were also concentrating on areas where our 2+2=5 concept might pay dividends. Included in all of our evaluations were observations that would determine how well the cultures of the two companies might blend together.

We decided also not to meet as a group but to split up for a broader look at Northrop, using the time we had to the greatest advantage. Denien would evaluate their aircraft programs, Anderson would evaluate their technical and scientific capability, and I would look hard at their business practices, strategies and administrative challenges. Three days seemed a short time for these evaluations, but at this point both companies were only still evaluating their options.

We received a very thorough series of presentations covering a broad range of programs and company procedures. Each of us was able to spend a good deal of time with our counterparts, not only getting a broad picture but also getting into some detail about future opportunities.

At the end of this visit we had the opportunity to meet with Northrop's CEO, Kent Kresa to exchange our thoughts about possible future business arrangements. At this meeting we made it clear to Mr. Kresa that we were not considering any form of acquisition but we were interested in some form of combination of the two companies. Kresa reacted positively to that approach and we agreed to meet again in the near future.

On the return trip to New York, we had some very intense discussions about a possible Northrop-Grumman merger. It was not our job to make any specific merger decisions. That would start with Renso Caporali, Bob Myers, and Bob Anderson. For the first time in our discussions and deliberations, we suddenly felt the emotions that this was for real and there was a strong possibility that Grumman was about to change forever. None of us was really in favor of a major change to the company but we also knew enough about the future of the defense business to realize that it was going to have to happen and it had to be very soon, since our options were running out. Up to now it had been only analysis and evaluation, but now it was decision time. We all three agreed that our recommendation would be for continued serious discussions. It was time for our team to make a strong recommendation to Caporali about Northrop as a partner. The recommendation would be to continue to move forward in a positive direction with Northrop.

Caporali and his top team heard our report and decided that it was appropriate to brief the Board of Directors on all of our activities. That briefing was scheduled for the upcoming board meeting and I presented the Board with a complete history of all of the work done by the "Project X" team, and the results of discussions that we and Caporali had had with Boeing and E Systems, along with a complete look at the future of defense business. The Board, of course, had been kept informed of the F-14 decisions and was well aware that future defense business would not support Grumman as a stand-alone defense prime contractor. At this point there was no decision required of the Board concerning any specific merger because we were not yet at that point. They were, however, made aware by Caporali that we were moving rather rapidly in the direction of a merger with someone.

Soon after the first Board briefing, Caporali and Kresa had another conversation and agreed that both companies could move forward with more detailed evaluations, specifically leading to some form of merger of the two companies. It was made clear by both CEO's that moving forward did not mean that a decision had been made, only that we should go forward with more detailed discussions.

Chapter Six

Handshakes, Commitments and Non-Commitments

After nearly a year of meetings and discussions between my team and the Northrop team, the CEO's of both Grumman and Northrop agreed that we could begin serious discussions that could lead to a possible merger. Both Boards of Directors had been briefed on our activities. I had been Grumman's team leader of this work from the beginning and Renso Caporali asked me to continue in this role. Jim Roche, my counterpart at Northrop was also selected by Kent Kresa to represent Northrop in these continued discussions. Roche and I had by now developed a high level of respect for each other. We had met several times and talked by phone frequently during the days and weeks between our meetings, but now it was time for serious discussions to move events forward. A possible merger was a reality, although no formal commitments had been made by the CEO of either company. Both Roche and I felt that it was now time for something other than a general agreement to continue study of merger possibilities. It was time for the top three leaders of both companies to get together and make a final commitment.

It was mid December of 1993 and Jim Roche and I had done everything we could think of to understand each other's company. We had gathered and exchanged a great deal of information, that under some circumstances would have been considered due diligence. Both Roche and I had briefed our respective Boards of Directors on our progress. We had put together several of the top executives in their respective divisions to get aquainted and now it was time for the companies top leaders and decision makers to get together for the final agreement to move forward with the merger.

I arranged for a room at the Garden City Hotel, on long Island. It was a cold and rainy night, but the weather was secondary on everyone's mind. I accompanied Renso Caporali, Bob Myers, and Bob Anderson to Garden City, but it was not my intention to join them in the meeting, only to make any necessary introductions.

Kent Kresa arrived with his team, which included Richard Waugh, Northrop's Vice president for Finance and Richard Molleur, Northrop's Legal Counsel. The six men were together for about an hour. For the first time in nearly a year, discussions were being held about merging the two companies and I had no idea what was being said. I received no briefing from the meeting, only the comment from Caporali that everything had gone fine and we should continue to get more detailed on the financial arrangements for a merger of equals.

Roche and I talked on the phone the next day, both feeling a little funny about the results of the meeting. We had expected a final, strong go ahead from our leaders which would move us into the final phase of the merger, but neither of us got that direction. It was strange to me but apparently not quite as strange to Roche. He indicated that it was Kresa's style to withhold final decisions on important subjects like this until he was absolutely convinced that the right decision was being made. Roche also indicated that Kresa rarely showed any premonition when making important decisions. Roche felt that the nod he got to continue moving forward was enough of a signal to continue our efforts.

We both, Roche and I, had military experience although his was a career and mine was a service term. We had both been military officers which carried an automatic level of respect for each other. In terms of raw intelligence, I gave Roche a significant edge but that had never bothered me in the past. It was obvious to both of us that we were both well respected in our respective companies, and our similar positions put us in a good advisory position with the top company leadership. We both reported directly to our respective CEO's and we both felt that we had their complete confidence and trust in our management skills.

With all of the respect that I had developed for Roche, I felt that I had to be cautious because of his very dominant personality. He was physically a big man with a somewhat intimidating style. He could alternate between charm and anger with ease. On the other hand I never considered myself a big guy, at 5'9" I was accustomed to looking up at the faces of my associates and I felt that I could also easily alter my form of interface. I had never been considered a charming guy myself, nor was I ever easy to work for. I had always demanded results from my subordinates and I measured myself by those same standards. There was no doubt in my mind that Jim Roche and I were going to be compatible associates in this very important continued assignment.

Apparently both Renso Caporali and Kent Kresa felt the same way about Roche and me because they both agreed to have us dedicate full time to leading the future discussions of a possible consolidation of the two companies. Our direction was to look hard for reason for the two companies not to get together, and to look intelligently and without bias at the positive reasons for a future merger. We both recognized the enormous responsibility that came with the task that we had been handed. We were to carefully evaluate all possibilities and bring our recommendations to our respective managements that would alter the future of both companies. We both recognized the significance of this assignment.

There were those more emotional times when we confided in each other that neither of us really wanted to change the nature of our companies, but we both knew, as well as many other defense industry executives, the end of an era had come and we had no choice but to respond to it. Grumman had already published its strategic statement shifting its emphasis to electronic system integration and information systems. Admitting that it could no longer maintain its core competence in aircraft design was a heart-wrenching decision for Grumman, but one that needed to be made. Northrop's aircraft capability had been bolstered by winning the B-2 competition, but the cut backs in that program and its eventual termination would place Northrop in a similar position relative to aircraft development and production. Northrop had an advantage that it had negotiated a contract for the B-2 which would permit the company to recover significant amounts of capital investment cash if the program did not produce the originally agreed-to number of aircraft. Those contract terms were already in effect, putting Northrop in a strong financial position for future growth. Kent Kresa had quietly made it known that he felt that the best bet for Northrop was to convert the company core competence toward becoming a manufacturer of integrated systems, combining improved sensors and surveillance capabilities, long range precision strike and battle management computer networks.

With these changes in corporate direction, some already stated and others quietly understood, Roche and I were well aware that a Northrop-Grumman merger would provide a strong core competence toward achieving those objectives. We also knew that a merger by itself would not be the end product of our work. To obtain and retain a position among the top defense contractors, even a merged Northrop-Grumman would have to go further to build additional capability. We promised each other to work hard to help build the strong foundation for that future company.

We decided that our next planning meeting should take place in New York. Roche had not had the opportunity to visit Grumman yet and we felt that a visit and tour was a good background for the final planning discussions.

The purpose of this New York meeting was to lay out our plans for future discussions and determine how we would proceed from here to a final decision point. I picked Jim up at his hotel and we proceeded to Ruth's Chris Steakhouse for dinner. It was a long evening, much more complicated that either of us had expected. After dinner and some fine wine, we both opened up to each other about events that were about to transpire. Northrop management was ready for a merger and although reluctant, so was Grumman's management. We now knew that this was not just another exercise, it was serious and the future of both companies was in our hands. That was a serious realization for both of us.

Since we both had essentially the same job in our respective companies, with minor differences, I felt that there might be an ethical problem that could arise if a merger took place. We would be putting together a merger plan knowing that at the corporate level, one of us would be planning himself out of a job. I felt that this could eventually lead to some bias on the part of one of us that might not be in the best interest of either company. I had a solution. I suggested that to avoid this possible dilemma, I would promise, if a merger was accomplished, to retire after it was all put together. This would take away any possibility of personal bias. I was 58 at the time, but Roche was considerably younger. I felt that it was time to hand the baton to the younger generation and I would step down at the time of the merger. Over a glass of Merlot, I reached across the table and we had a handshake on that decision. It may seem strange to many that a promise such as that was really important, but to the two of us, it solidified our deep-seated trust in one another, a trust that has continued long after the events of the combination of the two companies. When we shook hands, we both had a tear in our eye knowing that we were about to do something special.

Because of rules and procedures of the Securities and Exchange Commission, both Roche and I and I and our teams were all required to sign non-disclosure statements that prevented any of us from participating in stock trading of either company going forward. We were also not permitted to disclose to others outside the immediate teams, any of what was taking place in our merger talks.

Also during this first Roche visit to Grumman, we laid out the plan for moving forward. In summary it included the following.

1. The financial experts of both companies would prepare valuations of their respective companies. This information would be exchanged openly.

2. A detailed evaluation of the existing contracts of each company would be documented to insure that none of the existing programs under contracts would in any way be jeopardized by a merger.

3. Each company would define its core competencies and those advanced programs designed to extend those competencies.

4. Each company would provide details of its internal organizations and the key people in all significant areas.

5. Capital investments would be evaluated in terms of availability for future programs.

6. Benefits analysis would be conducted by each company and compared to insure that these benefits would not interfere with each other.

7. A detailed analysis would be performed of the geographic locations of all plants and facilities, with emphasis on possible consolidations.
8. Organizational analysis would be performed aimed at a preliminary determination of possible future cost savings
9. A detailed shareholder value analysis would be performed of a combined company to determine if a merger was in the best interest of the shareholders.
10. A legal review would be conducted to insure that there was a complete understanding of any legal issues, law suits or other legal obstacles that might prevent a combination of the two companies.

Northrop was slightly ahead of us in the acquisition process since they had just come off of a lost competition with Lockheed for the acquisition of General Dynamics Tactical and Military Aircraft Division. The General Dynamics bid was high on Northrop's strategic acquisition list because it would have given them most of the F22 and F16 production along with the new stealth fighter.

General Dynamics was owned by the Crown Family with Henry Crown the largest shareholder. When he died in August of 1990, it became obvious that the Crown family was going to shed the company from its holdings. Kent Kresa had set his sights on General Dynamics. If he was successful with the acquisition, it would provide the company some insurance of remaining a serious military aircraft supplier. When the company was finally put on the market in 1992, it was split into different sections in order to draw broader attention. Northrop was concentrating on the Military Aircraft Production sector. Since this was one of Norhrop's first large acquisition attempts, there was some differing strategy being recommended within the company. One strategic recommendation suggested that the sale would be a one shot opportunity. This was based on the theory that the Crown family simply wanted a clean and simple sale without any drawn out auction. Because of this possibility, Roche was suggesting that Northrop make its best offer right from the start. The other internal strategy suggested that Northrop withhold its best offer for a second round of bidding. Unfortunately when the bids were opened, the one shot approach was used and the Lockheed bid was accepted for $1.5 billion. Northrop was prepared to counter with another offer but it was not accepted. Northrop found itself left behind in this competition. This experience however really set the stage for the activity with Grumman. After the error in strategy that caused Northrop to lose the General Dynamics competition, Kresa started to lean more heavily on the strategy advice of Jim Roche, so I knew that when dealing with Roche, he was working from recent, although not a successful, experience.

We also knew that there was an important time table attached to our work. Martin Marietta had recently purchased the General Electric Aerospace Division for $3 billion. There were also rumors of discussions between Martin and Lockheed. Raytheon was moving rapidly to become a serious threat with its acquisition strategy. There was an atmosphere of urgency for action throughout the defense industry. Despite the intensity of merger and acquisition activity surrounding us, we were determined to take our time and thoroughly study our options.

The Culture Issue

One of the qualitative factors that always quietly overshadowed our deliberations was the culture of the two companies. This was a very difficult area to evaluate because it could not easily be reduced to a numerical measurement. From the beginning of Grumman's history, the company was known for its paternalistic orientation toward its employees. The company's open door policy, which was sometimes difficult to manage, made every employee feel that he or she had access to management at all times. The company's pay policy was based on individual merit rather than simply using some federal index to determine raise policy. Both of these policies were controversial but proved successful over the long run.

The company's benefits package included medical insurance, a pension plan, life insurance, disability insurance, both short and long term. All of these benefits were completely paid for by the company. Some of the more informal benefits included vacation and paid absence time and with careful planning, paid time off between the Christmas holidays. For much of the company's history the employees received a turkey at Christmas and both Christmas and Thanksgiving bonuses based on company performance.

There were other programs for the employees like the tuition refund program, the company newspaper (Plane News), and annual company picnic that was attended one year by 47,000 people. The company's athletic association (GAA) sponsored 35 different clubs and activities.

One benefit that is often overlooked was the company's attitude toward family relationships. For many years, each summer Grumman would hire hundreds of the sons and daughters of its longer term employees. The philosophy was that if the parent had a good work ethic and was a good employee, chances are that the child would have those same values. Hundreds of these summer employees were eventually hired back as full time employees after their schooling was completed. For many years Grumman gave a limited number of College scholarships to engineering students that showed great promise. Many of these scholars returned to the company upon graduation and became a critical part of the company's technical base and many moved upward into management positions. For its entire history Grumman remained a non –union company. This fact spoke well for the satisfaction of the employees that the company was concerned about employee interests.

In 1980 the company conducted a comprehensive survey of more than 1300 employees to determine their attitude toward the company. Two members of the faculty of The Stony Brook University were brought in to manage this survey. The results showed that the work culture, benefits and attitudes of the employees reflected positively toward the company's employment policies. The word choices that the employees made that best represented their attitude toward the company were; quality products, benefits, company pride, kindness and job security.

The attitudes reflected in the survey were embedded in all of the employees. As people gained experience and moved upward into management positions, all of the positive attributes of the company were translated into loyalty. Professional employees were never asked to punch a time clock, and conversely, when the job demands required long hours to address a problem or meet a schedule, everyone worked as necessary, often without compensation. Rarely was there any question as to either employee loyalty to the company, or the company's loyalty to its employees.

The loyalty question became an issue in the years between 1969 and 1977. As the Apollo program drew to an end, Grumman was required to lay off more than 13,000 employees. The employment level dropped from 37,000 down to around 23,000. Management tried to manage these layoffs by releasing small numbers each week so as not to flood the local job market. This was the first time in Grumman's history that the company had to make a reduction in its work force of any significant magnitude. Also, for the first time, the loyalty question became an issue.

Because most of the upper management of the company were long term employees who had worked their way up through the ranks, they were aware of the business environment that existed at the time of our merger studies. Most of management had worked through the era of the A-6, E-2 and F-14 aircraft programs. They had felt the joy of the moon landing and took a great deal of pride in all of the company's programs. The loyalty of the company's management was a factor that was considered very important toward making any merger a success.

To many outside the walls of the company, the attitude of the Grumman employees was sometimes puzzling. Up until the 1990's, more than 200,000 employees had walked through the doors of the company. Every one of these employees instantly became a member of the Grumman family and developed the Grumman attitude of pride. Why wouldn't they? The company took care of their health care, paid for the birth of their children, educated their families and paid everyone a decent wage for the work they performed.

If a merger was to be consummated, company loyalty would play a big part toward a successful and rapid integration of the two companies. While at the Northrop facilities, our Grumman evaluation team spent a lot of time trying to observe any differences that might exist in the attitudes of the employees toward the company. Cursory evaluations showed that company benefits were approximately the same and the attitudes of the people seemed to show the same product loyalty that we had witnessed at Grumman. We perceived a slight difference in the work ethic which we attributed to the "west coast ethic" versus the "east coast ethic". This could be observed by the apparent strict adherence to the quitting time, especially on Fridays. Other than that peculiarity, there appeared to be no reason for concern about different cultures hampering any possible combination of the two companies.

Chapter Seven

The Time Has Come For a Merger

Nearly a year of detailed discussions had taken place between my team and the team at Northrop. There was little more that we could do in terms of finding potential problems or developing synergies between the two companies. It was now time to start formal merger procedures and define financial arrangements and organizational structure. Before we could move forward with those activities, it was necessary for our Boards of Directors to conduct the final review and insure that all of the legal matters were in order to proceed with final merger activities.

There are different memories of different versions of events that took place. There are subtle differences of opinion here so I will attempt to fairly represent all sides. There are my own memories, many of which were documented in my files. I had spent the better part of the last year working on this Grumman-Northrop merger so I feel that my memory of events is not clouded. Then there is the record of the Board of Directors, which I suppose is the legal definition of what events took place during those last three or four months. Perhaps the difference in the two versions is the time I spent in the Board Room making presentations and listening to the discussions that followed and the activities of the Board when I was not in that room. It is not unusual for there to be two different versions of these events. After all, I was only the reporter bringing the facts to their attention. There was certainly a great deal of discussion during their actual deliberations that I would not have been privileged to hear. It would not be unusual if some members of the Board of Directors, having heard all of my presentations about the Northrop merger, might feel that I was possibly too close to the situation to view it fairly. I can understand that feeling. Like every other Grumman executive involved in these activities, I hoped that there would be another solution to our situation that would keep the company as it always had been. But I had been very aware of the speed with which things were happening around us that dictated we move forward in some meaningful direction. Having done all of the studies, I knew that a friendly merger with Northrop was the best alternative that we had available to us at that time. I certainly must have shown that enthusiasm in my most recent presentations to the Board. To insure fairness in my presentation, I will present both versions of the events that followed.

It was the 21st of January, 1994 and the Grumman Board was meeting for its regular monthly meeting at Grumman. This meeting was to be different because it was to include the final report on our work with Northrop and hopefully a vote to approve moving ahead with the merger. Because of the significance of the material at this meeting, there were certain formalities that needed to be addressed. First, there was the need for a legal review by an independent legal firm to insure the Board that all of the necessary legal matters had been properly addressed. Second, the Board needed to hear the opinion of an Investment Banking firm to assure that a merger was in the best financial interests of the shareholders. Goldman Sachs had been hired months earlier to work with my team and follow our deliberations and make the necessary financial valuations and comparisons. Gene Sykes, the Goldman lead person in these activities had worked with us for some time, and joined me at this Board meeting to endorse our findings and recommendations. All of the material planned for presentation at this meeting was reviewed with Sykes in advance. I expected the meeting to go as smoothly as the previous briefing meeting had gone.

Several months earlier when a merger seemed apparent between Grumman and Northrop, both companies signed confidentiality agreements because they were about to exchange non-public financial data. When Goldman Sachs was hired in late 1993 to work with us, they agreed to a sum of $250,000 to assist with the financial evaluations, and of course, it was assumed their agreement also called for strict confidentially toward the work we were doing.

The meeting was opened by Chairman Caporali and after some quick formalities, he informed the Board that we were going to make our final presentation about our Northrop work that would hopefully lead to Board approval of a merger. He also informed the Board of some of the formalities that were necessary, including an outside legal review and confirmation of the financial status by our Investment Banker.

My presentation lasted about 30 minutes and contained a summary of all of the work that we had done leading to our conclusion that a merger with Northrop was our best choice at the time. There was nothing in my report that was considered new or shocking, only a review of data that the Board had already seen. There were no apparent concerns expressed while I was at the podium.

Next was the endorsement by the outside legal firmTom Genovese had hired to review all of the legal steps that had been or needed to be taken. The lawyers reported no problems with the merger.

Caporali solicited comments from Board members and I remember none that were significant. As a final matter Caporali asked for the opinion of the Investment Banker.

Sykes, seated beside me, indicated that Goldman Sachs had reviewed our work and found it to be sound. He added however that Goldman Sachs felt that before Grumman proceeded with a merger with Northrop, we should take another look at Martin Marietta. At that point he produced a book detailing the Martin Marietta information, much of which we had reviewed previously.

I expect that my face must have turned white with shock! I never remember in my professional career feeling that I had been betrayed, but that was the feeling that I had at that moment. "Where did this come from," I thought. Caporali's direction to me months earlier was to keep all of our work very confidential so that our studies would not turn into a hostile takeover. With one short statement by Goldman Sachs, under contract to Grumman, that confidentially was about to be blown, opening us to an acquisition offer by anyone interested. This was exactly what we had worked so hard to prevent. Since I had no other material to present to the Board, I was dismissed and left the Board Room. Later I ran into Sykes in the hallway and asked him what the hell had happened. His only response to me was something like, "sometimes these things happen in corporate dealings."

Everything I have presented is fact as I remember it. From the time the Board Room door closed behind me, little did

I know that I was about to be shut out of everything that happened for the next two weeks.

Meanwhile, back in Northrop headquarters in Los Angeles, Kent Kresa, Northrop's CEO, was waiting for a call from Caporali indicating that the Board had agreed to move forward with the merger. When that call never came, Kresa had Jim Roche call me for details. Since I was not under any obligation to tell anything but the truth, I told them of the Goldman statement about Martin Marietta. When Kresa was told by Roche, he was also so shocked that he called me to make sure that Roche had not heard me incorrectly. I told Kresa that I assumed that Caporali was as shocked as I was and I had no knowledge of what the next step was to be. I had heard nothing from Caporali and was given no direction as to a further review of Martin Marietta.

We all went home for the weekend and when returning to work the following week, the news broke that Martin Marietta had offered to buy Grumman for $55 per share. Like magic, almost overnight, this large company had done its homework enough to be ready to make that offer to buy Grumman. I couldn't help thinking, what's wrong with us? We took nearly a year to come to the decision to merge with Northrop and Martin Marietta comes along in a couple of days and offers to buy Grumman. Something was all wrong. In my mind, it just does not happen that fast.

I was told that a team from Martin Marietta would be available to start their due diligence on February 8th in New York City and I should have my team available there to coordinate those studies. The work was to be done in an un-named office complex on Park Avenue that was leased by Goldman Sachs. This gave me the hint that Goldman was also under contract to Martin Marietta for their acquisition of Grumman. It just didn't smell right to me, but, as good soldiers, we assembled a team for the Martin Marietta due diligence.

I was told nothing by my management about any conversations that were held with Martin Marietta. In a due diligence procedure, my obligation was to present whatever data was requested by Martin, and to accommodate any meeting that they wished to have with Grumman personnel in areas of interest to them.

The lead executive for Martin Marietta during all of the due diligence discussions was Bill Teiken, a former General Electric executive. Martin had acquired the General Electric Aerospace Division in November of 1992 for approximately $3 billion. The deal involved $2 billion in cash and $1 billion in convertible preferred stock. That purchase increased Martins revenue from about $6 billion to more than $11 billion and increased their employee base by more than 33,000 people. Our intelligence indicated that in the two years since that acquisition, the GE organization had been swallowed up within Martin.

I described earlier in this book that our Project X studies had one element that looked for 2+2=5 synergies between interested companies, meaning that the total of a combined company would have to equal more than the sum of the individual parts.

I found it interesting when researching for this book, that when the GE acquisition was announced, Jack Welch, the CEO of General Electric Corporation, made the statement that the two companies fit together like achieving a 1+1=3 where the combination would produce results that were greater than either of the companies could produce on their own. He indicated that the additional strength of the combined company would permit them to enter competitions that neither would have been capable of entering alone. This was the exact concept that our team had presented for a Grumman-Northrop merger. GE had apparently been well integrated into Martin. The due diligence team sent to New York by Martin appeared to me to be largely former GE personnel. I initially thought this to be a little strange. It almost seemed like Martin had sent in its second team to perform the due diligence,

As the week progressed, I didn't sense any passion on the part of Martin to complete a successful acquisition of

Grumman. The activities were very well organized. The work tasks had been broken down into specific organizational groups and Martin had defined specific data requirements and formats to be supplied by each Grumman group. We received a schedule of briefings at least a day early so we could have the right people come into the city as defined by the schedule. Everything was very nicely laid out for us.

At the end of each day, my Grumman team reviewed everything that had been discussed. It looked to our people like the discussions were built around verifying that the valuation of Grumman would support the $55 per share offer.

At the conclusion of the Martin due diligence, things again happened rather quickly, again without my knowledge or involvement. It was announced that Grumman had accepted Martin's offer of $55 per share. Norm Augustine, Martin CEO, almost immediately came to Grumman and addressed a group of Grumman management personnel indicating that he had purchased Grumman. The atmosphere among Grumman personnel was complete shock. I kept asking myself, how could this happen so fast?

Meanwhile Kent Kresa was not sitting by quietly. He knew that his people had worked hard for a year putting together a plan that would result in a very successful merger of the two companies. Of course the financial conditions were now very different. A merger with Grumman would simply have been an agreement on the equalized share value of the combined company. Now as a hostile acquisition, the financials for Northrop were significantly different. Northrop was in a fairly good financial position with readily available cash. There was some concern expressed among Kresa's advisors about an outright acquisition but Kresa was determined to make a Grumman deal work. There had been some media reports that Kresa and his management team appeared not to be taking an aggressive approach toward seeking out new acquisitions. The actions of the next few weeks proved that to be untrue. On March 23, showing some anger, Kresa proposed a $60 per share offer to buy Grumman. Kresa indicated that if Grumman accepted his offer immediately, he would extend it to $62 per share.

At this point I'll have to do a short flash back to that January Board meeting. From my research and prodding of memories it seems that after I left the Board room there was direction given to both Renso Caporali and Goldman Sachs. The Board directed both parties to contact Martin Marietta to determine if they were interested in discussing a possible combination of some form. This contact could possibly trigger a series of unwanted hostile takeover offers, but the Board felt that we had to insure that we had made the best possible decision.

I suspect that Goldman Sachs needed to make no additional contact since I believe they were already in contact with Martin. Chairman Caporali called Norm Augustine and informed him that we had been looking over potential merger candidates and inquired as to Martin's interest in having discussions toward that direction. Apparently, Augustine not only confirmed his interest, but put forth an offer to buy Grumman for $55 per share cash. There were, however, conditions to his offer. First it was conditional upon a successful due diligence study. Second Augustine didn't want to enter an auction with Northrop so his offer needed to be accepted immediately. To insure that Northrop was excluded, Augustine added a third party clause to his offer indicating that once his offer was accepted, if a third party (like Northrop) entered with a bid and it bettered his offer, Grumman would be obliged to pay a penalty fee of $50 million to Martin.

I suspect that the third party penalty was not well known to the people who reviewed Martin's offer because it would have appeared to be a big incentive not to have the Board approve his offer without first consulting Northrop. Without concern for that penalty, the Board apparently felt that the Martin offer was acceptable and approved it without considering a possible Northrop counter offer.

Now moving forward, with Northrop now back in the game, the Grumman Board decided that it should offer both companies the opportunity to make a best and final offer to acquire Grumman. On March 28, 1994 Renso Caporali sent a letter to both companies outlining the rules for this competition. Significant abstracts from this letter follow.

"It is the strongly held view of the Board of Directors that this process must be conducted in an open, fair and orderly manner. The interest of our shareholders, employees, customers, suppliers and community and the public generally can and will be best served by such an approach. The Board of Directors is mindful that the process in which the Company is currently engaged does present certain risks, particularly if the process is prolonged, including disruption to the Company's business and overall uncertainty among the Company's constituencies as to the Company's future. In order to mitigate these risks, the Board of Directors believes that the most prudent course of action is to bring this process to a prompt and orderly close."

The letter goes on to establish the rules and procedures for submission of proposals. The rules essentially established 5:00 pm on March 31, 1994 as the deadline for final submissions and also stated that the offers would be held valid until April 4, 1994 at 9:00 am.

By this time, all kinds of mutterings and misleading reports were circulating among Grumman's employees. There were many rules in place that prevented telling the employees anything of what was going on, but Caporali was convinced that some form of communications with Grumman's employees was in order. On March 29, 1994 he released a letter to all employees. The contents of that letter are shown below.

"Fellow Grummanites:

"It seems that just when we most need to communicate, we are least able to do so. With competing tender offers for Grumman shares, we are in a complicated situation with no easy answers. Our direct communication with our shareholders right now is quite limited- and many Grumman employees are also shareholders, which makes matters worse. Many Grumman people are upset and angry that no one is talking to them. They resent reading about their company in the newspapers instead of hearing it first at work.

"If you've been following the accounts in the media, you won't see much that is attributed to a Grumman source: the legal ramifications of a misstatement are considerable. For the most part, comment is made by the two companies competing to acquire us, or by investment companies or other interested parties. When we do have something to say, we have legal obligations to make a public announcement and make sure that information is distributed to all outlets at the same time. This is done through press releases and filings with the Securities

and Exchange Commission. We are simply forbidden to single out one group of shareholders—our employees—for special communications.

"The uncertainty and the silence have been stressful for Grumman people. We still have products to build and services to perform for our customers, and the ongoing situation is disruptive to people's lives and to the work environment. For this reason, we asked Martin Marietta and Northrop to submit their best and final offers by Thursday, March 31. We hope to announce the winning bid by Monday morning, April 4."

"We appreciate your hard work, your patience and understanding during this very difficult time."

Still annoyed by the best and final procedure, Northrop submitted a letter to Grumman the next day, extending its offer to $62 per share if the offer was accepted within the next two days. If the offer was not accepted in that time frame it would revert back to the original $60 per share value. Grumman rejected that offer based on its letter asking for a best and final on March 31, 1994.

On April 5, 1994 it was announced that Northrop had increased its bid to $62 per share and Martin Marietta had held to its original bid of $55 per share. Northrop was declared the winner on April 5, 1994

The Grumman Investment Fund agreed to sell its Grumman stock to Northrop on April 12 and all other Grumman stock was tendered to Northrop on April 15, 1994.

During the first week of May, 1994, Northrop did its due diligence and all of the final arrangements were completed on May 18, 1994.

At the time that all of this corporate positioning was taking place, there were many questions that came to the surface. One big question was why, after taking such an aggressive action to interrupt months of negotiation between Northrop and Grumman, did Martin Marietta seemingly back away at the last minute without a fight. Press documents suggested that Norm Augustine did not have complete support from some of his executive advisors, feeling that his $55 offer in itself was too high a premium price to pay for Grumman. Other undisclosed sources say that Martin Marietta and Lockheed were already in preliminary discussions about getting together themselves. It was hinted later that one of the two parties might have suggested that they let Northrop get Grumman, integrate the two companies and then Martin and Lockheed would get together later, offering to merge with or buy Northrop Grumman. In retrospect, this does not sound too unreasonable because in 1996 there was an attempt for Lockheed Martin and Northrop Grumman to get together. Both companies agreed but the government would not approve the merger. Isn't it strange how these so called rumors have a way of gaining credibility?

The events of January and February of 1994 have bothered me for more than twenty years. I understand that I was only the leader of a team that worked on the merger of the two companies. My job was to do the studies, have the discussions, develop the relationships and hand my team's recommendations to my management. They were the ones that were to make the decisions. There needed to be a great deal of trust and confidence on both sides of this arrangement. For nearly all of the months that had transpired when merger discussions were taking place, that trust and confidence seemed apparent to me. My lesson in life, however, was that when the Board Room doors close, it's a different world behind them. Directors of every company have an obligation to represent the shareholders of that company and to insure that the actions of management also represent the best interests of those shareholders.

People who are selected to be outside Directors of a company usually are people of significant business or social standing with years of experience in their respective areas of expertise. It is expected that these people offer their expertise collectively so that debate and deliberation will result in the best possible decisions for the company. With individuals of this standing in life and in the community, there are often serious egos that are also represented. Board positions in companies the size of Grumman or Northrop, are not jobs or careers, but they are positions that come with a certain degree of prestige and also some financial reward. The possibility of losing a long held board position due to a merger or a hostile acquisition has to be a difficult pill for any board member to swallow. I don't know, nor am I implying, that any member of Grumman's Board of Directors were in any way effected by, or their decisions altered, by the hectic events of January and February of 1994. I do feel however that things happened very rapidly during those last days and weeks and when events take place that rapidly, it leaves room for mistakes to be made in the decision process.

I can say with complete confidence that my briefings of my team's activities before and during our deliberations with Northrop were presented to the Board in great detail. They were completely aware of every step that we had taken over a period of more than a year, leading to the final decision, outside the Board Room, to merge with Northrop. What really happened when I left the room and the Board Room doors closed, will forever remain a mystery to me.

The Facts on Record

During my discussions with Jim Roche, I often asked him to confirm some facts. We would talk about the events of 20 years ago and some voids in information that we both could not quite reconcile. We discussed the roles we played with our respective bosses and the confidence that they seemed to have in our ability. We both realized that we were the grunts that put it all together and made recommendations to the top brass, but they made the decisions and it was not necessary for us to always understand the logic of those decisions. Roche described it to me in a very descriptive manner by saying that he and I were the hunters and our bosses were the skinners. We brought in the meat and they took it all off the bone. This definition has stuck with me for a long time and perhaps it explains some of the things that happened in this history lesson. I have presented my memories but in fairness it is necessary to examine the documented record of the events of the last few months of Grumman's existence. The official record of these transactions are contained in the notes from the Board of Directors meetings as stated in the final proxy statement issued by the Board on May 3, 1994. I will not include the entire statement, but only those events that are pertinent to our discussion here. I will comment on areas that I feel are important relative to my previous discussion. The Board presents the background of the merger as follows:

"In light of past and anticipated decreases in military spending and consolidations in the defense/aerospace industries over the last several years and other market factors, the Board has

from time to time reviewed the Company's strategic planning, including the possibility of making acquisitions or entering into a business combination with a company engaged in similar related businesses. In late 1992, members of management of the Company had conversations with members of management of Northrop and others regarding the possibility of engaging in discussions related to a possible business combination, which discussions were brought to the attention of members of the Board. These conversations did not result in further discussions at that time. In early 1993, members of management of the Company and Northrop discussed again the possibility of a business combination between the companies. On January 21, 1993, the companies entered into a confidentiality agreement pursuant to which the companies exchanged certain confidential nonfinancial information, but did not engage in extensive discussions.

"In late December 1993, the Company retained Goldman Sachs & Company ("Goldman") as its financial advisor in connection with the Company's review of its strategic and financial alternatives.

"On January 20, 1994, a regular meeting of the Board was held to discuss among other things, the Company's strategic objectives. At the meeting, representatives of Goldman discussed with the Board various strategic alternatives, including growth of the Company through acquisitions as well as potential business combinations. Members of management discussed the status of

contacts between the Company and Northrop. Representatives of Goldman then discussed with the Board potential acquisitions, noting that it might be difficult for the Company to execute an acquisition strategy to achieve the critical mass necessary to compete effectively in its businesses while still achieving its financial objectives, and also analyzed and discussed a number of potential merger candidates. Representatives of Goldman also presented a review of a possible business combination between the Company and Northrop, including summary business and financial information and historical stock trading information about Northrop and an analysis of the related contributions of each company based on its sales, operating profit and free cash flow. At the conclusion of such meeting, the Board determined that it would be consistent with the Company's stated strategic objectives and the interests of the shareholders of the Company to continue to investigate possible acquisition opportunities as well as discuss other possible strategic alternatives for the Company."

Comment: In other words, despite a full year of study with the help of both the McKinsey group and Goldman Sachs, based on no new facts put forth, we should now take another look at Martin Marietta. A strange turn of events.

"In late January 1994, at the request of the Board, representatives of Goldman initiated contact with Martin Marietta Corporation ("Martin Marietta") to determine

if Martin had any interest in exploring a possible business combination with the Company."

Comment: Late January means the next week. That contact was made and Martin, without further study put forth an offer of $55 a share to buy Grumman.

"Between February 8 and February 15, 1994, representatives of the Company and representatives of Martin Marietta met and held discussions in connection with Martin Marietta's due diligence investigation of the Company. In the course of such investigation, the Company provided Martin Marietta with certain non-public information regarding the Company pursuant to a Confidentiality Agreement. During this period, Martin Marietta informed the Company that if there were business combinations between the companies, Martin Marietta would be able to provide maximum value to the shareholders of the Company in a cash transaction.

"On February 10, 1994, Northrop financial advisors presented representatives of Goldman with the outline of a possible stock-for-stock transaction which involved a cash election merger in which shareholders of each of the Company and Northrop would have the option to convert up to 34% of the shares of each company at an approximate 20% premium to market trading value and to exchange the remaining shares for shares of a new holding company on the basis of current market trading values.

"On February 17, 1994, the Board held its regular meeting at which management reviewed discussions with Martin Marietta and Northrop. Representatives of management discussed with the Board the respective capabilities of Martin Marietta and the Company as well as the potential benefits of a combination of the Company with Martin Marietta.................based upon, among other things, the presentations of representatives of management and Goldman, the Board then determined that it was not interested in pursuing a transaction with Northrop under the terms outlined in its proposal, and representatives of Goldman were asked to communicate that determination to Northrop."

Comment: Now after a year of detailed discussions with Northrop, Goldman Sachs representatives were handling all discussions with Northrop.

"On February 21, 1994, Martin Marietta sent the Company a letter stating that on the basis of the information provided to date, a projection of potential synergies and, subject to the conditions outlined therein, Martin Marietta would be prepared to place a cash value on shares of the Company of $55.00 each. Between February 23 and March 6, 1994 further negotiations and discussions were held between representatives of the Company and representatives of Martin Marietta, and as a result, the Company and Martin Marietta entered into an Agreement and Plan of Merger on March

6, 1994 ("the Martin Marietta Merger Agreement") which provides for the acquisition by Martin Marietta of all of the outstanding shares of the Company for $55.00 cash per share. As contemplated by the Martin Marietta Merger Agreement, on March 8, 1994, Martin Marietta commenced a $55.00 per share tender offer for all of the Company's outstanding Shares."

Comment: Without any further review by Grumman people, the Board approved an agreement that contained a severe penalty clause if a third party entered the picture and Grumman accepted a better offer, even if that offer was much better for its shareholders.

"On March 9,1994, Northrop sent a letter to the Company expressing a continued interest in acquiring the Company and stating that the Board of Directors of Northrop had authorized the acquisition of the Company at $60.00 pers. On March 14, 1994, Northrop commenced the offer for all of the Company's outstanding shares at $60.00 per share.

"On March 28, 1994, the Company sent a letter to Northrop and Martin Marietta setting forth rules and procedures for submitting proposals to acquire the Company, which provided among other things, that any proposal should be the bidder's best and highest offer" and should be delivered by 5:00PM. on March 31,1994. Each of Northrop's and Martin Marietta's

submittal letters to the Company by the deadline, with Martin Marietta indicating that it had no interest in increasing its $55.00 per share offer and Northrop indicating that it was prepared to increase its $60.00 per share offer to as high as $66.00 depending upon whether, and by what amount, Martin Marietta increased its offer.

"On April 2 and 3, 1994, representatives of Northrop and the Company met to discuss and negotiate the terms of the Merger Agreement, which thereafter was entered into on April 3. On April 4, Northrop announced that it had increased its price it was offering and amended its Offer to $62.00 per share in accordance with the terms of the Merger Agreement.

"On April 3, 1994, the Company's Board held a special meeting. At such meeting the Board reviewed with senior management, legal counsel and financial advisors the discussions and negotiations between the Company and Northrop since the last meeting of the Board.........recommending that the shareholders of the Company accept the Offer and tender their shares to Northrop and approve and adopt the Merger Agreement; authorizing the termination of the Martin Marietta Merger Agreement, including authorization of payment of the fee required thereby, and affirming that, in light of all the relevant circumstances, the Board recommended that the Shareholders reject the Martin Marietta tender offer.

"Northrop's Offer expired at 12:00 midnight on April 15, 1994 and as a result Northrop purchased all shares tendered pursuant thereto (37,766,109 shares or approximately 93.4% of the outstanding shares)."

Other Factors

As one can imagine, there was a great amount of dialog among Board members during all of the above events. The Proxy Statement referenced above also stated the terms of the Goldman Sachs arrangement with Grumman. On December 23, 1993, Grumman retained Goldman Sachs for a twelve month period to assist in our reviews of strategic alternatives. The fee for this activity was $250,000. On February 17, 1994, Grumman entered a second agreement with Goldman Sachs to have them provide financial advice in connection with possible strategic combinations that were about to take place. Goldman's fee for this activity was to be $10,778,129 plus reimbursement of several expense items. Press information that was made public after the merger was completed indicated that by cancelling the Martin Marietta merger agreement, Grumman was required to pay Martin Marietta a penalty fee of $50 million and an additional fee to Goldman Sachs for their efforts with Martin Marietta of about $8 million. In total Goldman Sachs earned close to $20 million for its efforts over a period of less than six months.

In preparation for the April 3, 1994 Board meeting, Goldman Sachs prepared a series of financial analyses to provide the Grumman Board comparisons of the relative value of the Martin Marietta offer of $55.00 per share and the Northrop offer of $62.00 per share. These analyses were very complete and used several different evaluation techniques to derive projected results. In summary their work showed that the Martin Marietta offer of $55.00 per share represented a premium of approximately 20% based on the variation of the high's and low's of the Grumman stock price over the last 12 months.

The same analysis showed that the Northrop offer of $62.00 per share represented a premium of 56% over the average stock price for the past twelve months and a premium of nearly 99% based on the low stock value during the same period.

Goldman also performed analyses to project what the new company's combined stock price would be for both Martin Marietta and Northrop once a merger was completed and the companies integrated. These findings were complicated and variable but showed little difference for either combination of companies.

Chapter Eight

Reaction Inside Northrop

The advantage of writing a book about historical events is the ability to flash back and look behind the scenes at events that have already taken place. When the first shocking offer was made by Martin Marietta, I could only imagine the disappointment being felt by many of the top executives at Northrop.

After nearly a year of detailed discussions with Northrop, I knew that their management would not take the news of the Martin Marietta interference lightly. Both Kent Kresa and Jim Roche had previously made it clear to me that they liked the Grumman heritage and wanted passionately to make it part of the Northrop family. Of course all of our discussions to date were directed toward a friendly merger of equals, so there was never any hostility associated with our discussions. During my first contact with both Kresa and Roche after the Martin Marietta announcement, I sensed anger for the first time from both men. Kresa made the simple statement that it was not yet over and Roche, perhaps allowing his military background to emerge, indicated that the battle was about to begin. I later learned that Roche had defined the next few weeks as the "Tora Tora Tora" phase of the fight for Grumman.

For those readers not yet old enough to recall the meaning of these words let me digress for a moment. In 1941 as the Japanese were preparing to attack Pearl Harbor, they appointed a Lieutenant Commander named Mitsuo Fuchida the leader of the airborne attack squadron. The planes commanded by Fuchida left their aircraft carriers about 200 miles west of Hawaii, and flew above the clouds toward their target. As Fuchida dropped below the clouds, he saw that the American aircraft carriers were not in the port, a significant disappointment to him. To his dismay however, many American battle ships were lined up along their moorings and these ships were the pride of the American Naval fighting force. He immediately sent the signal to the rest of the airborne force that the battle could commence. The pre-arranged signal for the attack was "Tora Tora Tora." The literal meaning of the word Tora was "tiger" but the acronym meant "lightning attack." These three words have been credited as the starting point for the United States entry into the Second World War.

Northrop seemed silent for a few days after the Martin Marietta announcement, but that apparent silence was the result of their battle planning. Northrop had been defeated in their previous attempt to acquire General Dynamics and I knew that Kresa was not going to lose face again. Several of Northrop's top management knew of the discussions that were being held between the two companies but for the most part those discussions were kept secret. Kresa sent a letter to Caporali announcing that Northrop was going to continue its efforts, but this time those efforts would be directed at an acquisition. As soon as Northrop received confirmation that Caporali had received the letter, Roche had a huge banner raised in the executive staff area with the words, "Tora Tora Tora." This was intended as the signal that the Northrop battle to acquire Grumman had begun. It was also a big morale booster for the staff members that had worked so hard to support our earlier efforts.

For two days after the battle signal was given, both Roche and Kresa would spend nearly every hour of those two days on the phones, putting a three-day rolling plan in place that would carefully keep everyone informed including politicians, press and media, and financial institutions. This plan was intended to stay in front of Martin Marietta's efforts to interrupt Northrop's year-long planning. Northrop's efforts in this regard were apparently successful. It was reported back to Northrop by a reporter, that Norm Augustine, Martin's CEO, had made the statement that Northrop's battle for Grumman should be considered "against our national security."

Despite Northrop management feeling dismayed and betrayed by Grumman's fast acceptance of Martin Marietta's offer, they decided to take a soft approach into the battle in an attempt to make what could be a very hostile battle less caustic. The Northrop battle plan considered each of the steps that Martin Marietta might take and they had a counter plan in place to immediately react to that action.

Kresa later told me that the only action that he could not counter was his deep disappointment that because of his long standing friendship with Grumman's CEO Caporali, he assumed that he would have been called by Caporali the instant Martin Marietta's name was thrown on the table at the January Board meeting. That call never came, hence the feeling of betrayal.

Chapter Nine

The Role of the Investment Banker

As I described the events leading up to the acquisition of Grumman by Northrop, my readers might sense that I don't feel very warm and fuzzy about the activities of our investment banker. As the events unfolded in 1994, there were several occasions where I began to develop suspicions about the effectiveness of our banking representative. During those hectic days and in the more than 20 years that have passed since, I have never had any absolute evidence that there was any wrong doing, but even today I am left with feelings of doubt.

There is an assumption of confidentially that goes along with the engagement of an investment banker. Goldman Sachs was brought on board under a formal agreement very early in our deliberations defining Grumman's future options. They did the work that we requested and provided valuable information about the financial strength and valuations of all of the companies that we evaluated. They participated in many of our study meetings and were fully aware of the companies that we might be courting, and also those we had ruled out. They had provided an evaluation of Martin Marietta as they did for all other companies we requested. To the best of my memory, they never expressed any positive opinion about Martin Marietta. Neither did they express any negative opinion about Northrop. When they accompanied me to the final Board meeting to present our recommendations concerning Northrop, they never gave me any indication that they were about to sabotage our choice of Northrop as a merger partner by recommending Martin Marietta as a possible contender.

From the time that Martin Marietta was introduced by Goldman Sachs, it was a matter of only a few days until Martin Marietta made a formal offer to acquire Grumman. It took us more than a year of intense study to decide on Northrop as a partner. How did Martin Marietta, apparently nearly over night, make the decision to acquire Grumman? Something is not right with this timing.

After the three days that I was excluded from all activities between Goldman Sachs and the Grumman Board of Directors, I kept asking, "What was the motivation to accept a Martin Marietta offer that contained language that would exclude Northrop from participating in any future auction, or, denying them the opportunity to make a counter offer?" "Why so fast?" I asked? Could it possibly have been that a merger between Northrop and Grumman would provide a lesser banking fee than would a hostile battle for Grumman?

I have determined from public records that Goldman Sachs received fees exceeding $28 million as a result of the activities previously described. This is certainly far greater than the $250,000 fee originally negotiated for financial analysis assistance or even the $10.7 million later agreed to, to help with merger financial evaluations. This is a substantial motivation to encourage a hostile take-over.

I have been asked many times during and since the Northrop transactions, why we needed an investment banker at all in the early stages of our studies? This is probably the only question that can be answered factually because I asked it myself.

I did considerable research on corporate mergers as we began our partnering deliberations. I discovered rather quickly that those mergers which succeeded financially in the past involved companies that had done one or more mergers previously. Those mergers which had failed were between companies engaging in a merger for the first time. Grumman had no recent merger history and we were all aware of the horrors associated with some of the company's past acquisitions. These mistakes were a large part of the reason why the company was in financial trouble. As a result, it was important to work side by side with an organization that had merger experience. One of the main roles of an investment banking firm in a merger or acquisition is to establish a fair market value for the companies involved in the transaction. We knew that we would be looking at a number of companies, both as acquisition or merger candidates. Proper valuation of these companies would probably play a significant role in determining the potential of any form of alliance.

Investment bankers are the experts at calculating what a business is really worth. They are able to predict how that worth would be altered under a number of different scenarios using proven financial models. Investment banks also often perform the service of arbitrage for their clients. This involves finding a target company that has a market value much lower than what the business is really worth. Merging with this type of company would offer the potential of much greater profit.

The investment banker's role in mergers and acquisitions generally falls into one of two categories: as a seller's representative or a buyer's representative. They are motivated to get a deal done because that is how they get paid. As a seller's representative, they attempt to get the highest sale price because their fee is based on that price. In a merger situation the fee of the investment bank is based on the value of the merged entity.

This is where the role of the investment banker gets a little fuzzy. In a merger of equals, the resulting company has an established value that is not really negotiated. If a merger turns into some form of hostile acquisition, the final successful bid price is usually driven higher than it might otherwise be valued by the bidding of two or more interested buyers. In this case the investment bank would make a much higher fee.

Some have speculated that this is exactly what happened when the merger of Grumman and Northrop suddenly turned into a hostile bidding war between Martin and Northrop. It appears that the organization that gained most from the acquisition was the investment bank. Of course this is only speculation.

Once we decided to proceed down the path of a merger with Northrop, the role of our investment banker was to insure that all of the financial analyses, synergy evaluations, and other business related studies were performed in a manner that provided truthful results for examination by the Board of Directors. The Board would be deciding for the shareholders on the advisability of the merger. The decision of the Board of Directors would certainly be heavily influenced by the recommendations of the Investment Bank advisor.

Twenty years have passed since that January 21, 1994 Board Meeting and barely a day has passed that I have not thought about the feeling of betrayal that I felt on that day. I have discussed the facts and events of those days with many people who were my associates at that time, to better understand what went wrong.

I have attempted to rationalize if there might have been one person in the Grumman organization who might have been motivated to leak word of our work to Martin Marietta. I do not believe that Martin could have come forth with their offer without first doing the same type of analyses that we were doing during our studies. This work takes time and would have required that Martin was tipped of our work and knew that Grumman would be vulnerable to a take-over.

I have tried to understand why a Board of Directors made up of seasoned and skilled business people, would have rushed to judgment and approved the Martin Marietta offer that contained very serious terms that, by its acceptance, ruled out any further discussion with Northrop without imposing a $50 million fine on Grumman.

In situations like this, it is usually wise to consider money as the single factor that drives these events. In this case it would have been the difference in the stock value had a merger been completed, versus the potential stock price if an acquisition was approved. The Martin offer of $55 per share was certainly a premium from where the Grumman stock was sitting at the time. Anyone with significant holding of Grumman stock would have preferred an acquisition over a merger, except perhaps members of Grumman's management who would likely lose their jobs with an acquisition,

Ruling out individuals, the one common thread to every aspect of this dilemma was Goldman Sachs. This organization had been privy to all of the work that our Project X team had done. They had conducted many value analyses for the study team as we narrowed out sights on Northrop. They were completely briefed on the recommendations that we were going to make to the Grumman Board and said nothing in advance of that briefing to indicate that they had another recommendation. Goldman Sachs was the banker that also authored the Martin Marietta offer, only days after the Board meeting, and they were also the banker that acted in behalf of Northrop in the final acquisition agreement. Goldman Sachs fees were greatly in excess of $28 million for their part with each of the involved companies. If one follows the money trail, it might seem as though Goldman Sachs made out better than any of the principals in this transaction. Instead of acting as an advisor/consultant, it appears Goldman Sachs was a player in the process, maximizing their fees at the expense of the merging parties.

Chapter Ten

The Sale is Complete, The Integration Begins

Once Northrop's final offer was accepted, the real challenge was to begin. The task was to find the most effective way to rapidly integrate the two companies. During the period of almost a full year that we had worked with Northrop hoping for a merger of equals, we had already done a good deal of this work. But now the situation was much different. It was no longer a cooperative effort to put two companies together in a friendly manner. As we somewhat humorously defined it, Northrop was the Buyer and Grumman was the "Buyee". It really wasn't funny at all. Many people on both sides of the debate had worked very hard to make this a friendly event. Somehow at the last minute things had suddenly changed. The task at hand was now a little more challenging.

Within hours after the Northrop offer was accepted by the Grumman Board, Kent Kresa called and asked me to come to Los Angles, this time not as a strategy planner, but as a potential employee. Kresa was aware of my handshake promise to Jim Roche, made months earlier, to retire as soon as the deal was done, but he was now asking me to stay on for as long as it took to put the two companies together. Kresa felt that since Roche and I had done most of the original synergy work, it made sense that we both be involved in the integration efforts. He asked Roche and me to be co-chairmen of the integration efforts.

I felt that Kresa was sincere in his intent to make this combination work as well as possible and I agreed to stay on for at least one year to help get the job done. Kresa also told me at the time he was very upset at not being informed immediately after the Board meeting of the Martin complication. He felt betrayed by those in Grumman's management who he considered his friends, feeling that he should not have been kept in the dark about the Martin intrusion, but should have received a call immediately after the Board meeting.

Kresa also informed both Jim Roche and me that he didn't feel the combination of Northrop and Grumman was the end game in the Defense sector. He expected additional combinations would be needed to keep his new company one of the top three defense companies. He suggested that while we worked together to integrate the two companies, we also work quietly together to define the next strategic steps that could be taken to continue to grow the company.

In a private meeting on a Friday evening in Kresa's office on the 19th floor of their headquarters building, a very significant question was asked of Jim Roche and me. Kresa indicated that for legal reasons, he would have to appoint a temporary head of the Grumman operations to handle the legal formalities of the transition. Kresa asked for our recommendation of who that person should be. Actually, Roche and I didn't need much time to think about our answer. Bob Denien had worked with us throughout the merger discussions and we both felt that he would be the best choice for that job. Denien was the Executive Vice president of the Aircraft Division and was thoroughly familiar with the inner working of Grumman. He was a well respected member of the executive team. After a lengthy discussion, Kresa seemed to agree with the Denien recommendation and both Jim Roche and I left the meeting feeling confident that the efforts in the months ahead to integrate the two companies would be smooth with Denien at the helm at Grumman.

Kresa also informed us that he knew we had both developed a strong friendship during the past year. He expected us to do everything in our power to see that our friendship caught hold throughout both companies. Kresa felt that the hostile acquisition could be turned into a friendly integration if it was approached that way by the leaders. We clearly understood that mandate.

I returned to New York the next day as planned. Keep in mind that in 1994, cell phones were not as ubiquitous as they are today, so communications were not as efficient. It was

Sunday afternoon when Roche called me at home to inform me that Kresa had been visited by some Grumman executive over the weekend and he had reversed his position on the temporary leadership. Whoever this Grumman executive was, he managed to convince Kresa that the temporary leader of Grumman should not be a career Grumman executive. Kresa had changed his mind and was appointing Olliver Boileau as the temporary head of Grumman.

Boileau was well known in the industry. He had been the leader of The Boeing Aerospace Company in 1980 and later that year he left to become the Vice Chairman of General Dynamics. He briefly retired after that assignment but came out of retirement to head Northrop's B-2 program. Boileau certainly knew the defense business, but he left behind him a reputation for being crude and dominating. His people management skills apparently left much to be desired. By Kresa's appointment of Boileau to head Grumman Operations, our job suddenly became much more difficult. From past reports, Boileau was a holy terror with people. We knew that to accommodate a smooth transition program, we would need the cooperation of the key people on both sides. Alienation of the people would complicate that task and Boileau had a reputation for being an alienator.

Shortly after the Boileau appointment, he moved to Long Island and decided to schedule a series of trips to all of

Grumman's outlying plants to welcome everyone to the new Northrop Grumman entity. I initially thought that this was a fine idea and a Gulfstream was scheduled for a series of trips in sequence to Milledgeville, Ga., Melbourne, St Augustine, and Stuart, Florida, then on to Lake Charles, Louisiana, Houston, Texas and finally out to our California plant in Ervine. This was to be my first experience with Boileau, and he had invited a few other Grumman management personnel to accompany us. The flight crew had scheduled an 8 am departure. The crew knew me well because of the number of trips to California that my team had made with them. The Gulfstream was to depart Republic Airport and the traffic on RT.110 was horrible that morning. At 8 am I was just approaching the airport and Boileau ordered the crew to close the door and depart without me. Clyde Stover of my staff was on the plane and he indicated to Boileau that I was just entering the complex. Boileau insisted that the flight crew close the door and depart. This was going to be his way to make his point to me about promptness.

The crew kept stalling, telling Boileau that there was a slight delay in our departure clearance and they could not taxi until that clearance was approved. I finally ran to the plane and hopped aboard and the door was closed. Boileau proceeded to chastise me like I was a small schoolboy, screaming that there was no excuse, including traffic for being late when he was in charge. His rant, in front of all of the other passengers went on for several minutes. This was my first encounter with Boileau, not a pleasant one.

When we arrived in Milledgeville, Boileau indicated that he wanted me to introduce him as the new President of Grumman. I was to say no more than that but I was to sit on the stage with him during the speech (rant) as a show of support. I honored his request and he began. It wasn't long after he started that I realized what a mistake this man was as a leader. He bragged about how many thousands of people he had laid off at Boeing and General Dynamics and how he would change Grumman forever. His threatening speech went on for a long time and by the time he finished I believe that every employee in the audience disliked him. Even more important, they were demoralized.

Back at the hotel that night I talked to him about the tone of his welcoming speech. I suggested that we were going to need the cooperation of these people to integrate the two companies and his ranting was not going to help. His response to me was that anyone who didn't cooperate would just be fired. He was now in charge and I should only attend to the job of integrating the two companies. He did however indicate that he would take a slightly softer tone at the next destination.

St Augustine, Florida was the next stop and although Boileau's tone was slightly less demanding, it still made the same points. Again I asked him to tone it down at the next stop and essentially he told me to mind my own business.

Next on the agenda was Melbourne, Florida. He wanted the same process, a short introduction and a show of my support by sitting behind him on the stage. Because this was a much bigger audience, he actually increased the extent of his rant indicating that any employee that didn't cooperate with the integration effort would be fired. The reaction among the Melbourne audience was obvious shock. These people were working on one of the most recent Grumman success programs, the JSTARS program. They certainly didn't expect this type of treatment from the company's "new leader."

Following the Melbourne meeting I called Kent Kresa and asked him to talk to Boileau. I briefed Kresa on the content of Boileau's speeches and expressed my feelings that he was turning every employee completely off on Northrop. Immediately after my call, Kresa called Boileau at the hotel and apparently told him of my concerns. Ollie went nuts. He came to my hotel room and said that he was going to fire me as soon as this trip was over. He felt that I had gone to Kresa behind his back and I should not have done that. I made it very clear that I did not go behind his back. In fact I had talked to him twice about his behavior before going to Kresa.

I also informed him that in my capacity as co-chairman of the integration activity, I worked directly for Kresa and not for him. I again reminded him that he was creating a terrible problem for himself with all of these employees. That didn't seem to bother him because as he indicated he was Ollie Boileau.

The next stop on this morale enhancing series of trips was Lake Charles, Louisiana where the production work was being done on the JSTARS airplanes. This time I made the introduction but I sat off of the podium stage. I had already decided if Boileau continued his rant, I was finished with the trip. Of course he bragged about how much he knew about manufacturing large aircraft and he would straighten out this production program. That night I called Ollie and told him that I would no longer accompany him on the remainder of the trip. I had booked a commercial flight back to New York the next morning and I was finished with his antics. He gave me no reaction except to hang up the phone on me. I flew to New York the next morning.

At this point I knew that Kresa's appointment of Ollie Boileau as the legal head of Grumman was a terrible mistake. In a very short time he had alienated thousands of Grumman employees. I believed that this was going to make it extremely difficult for Roche and me to complete our assigned task of completing a friendly integration the two companies. I spoke to

Kent Kresa shortly after my return to New York and suggested that it might be better if perhaps he appointed someone else to head the integration program because I just didn't want to deal with Boileau. Kresa asked me to stay on and try to avoid contact with Boileau if possible. I agreed to stay on as long as Boileau did not become an obstacle to our progress.

I had many interactions with Kent Kresa during the months we worked on merger details. He was always very professional and seemed very compassionate about relationships with employees. This appointment of Boileau seemed completely out of character for Kresa.

I was not really concerned about my ability to deal with Ollie Boileau. I had worked with many difficult people before. My real concern was the culture of the Grumman Company was very much people oriented. Grumman's open door policy was designed to hear out employee concerns, not to dominate them as though they were worthless. I had no intention of defending Boileau's actions. All I could do was try to make the Grumman people understand that Ollie Boileau did not represent the attitude of the rest of the Northrop management. The longer Bioleau continued at his job, the more difficult that task became for me.

Long after the integration of the two companies was completed, I asked Kent Kresa why he had made the decision to use Boileau as the temporary head of Grumman. Kresa said that Boileau was the only executive in Northrop that had the experience of running a large company. He was hired at Northrop for that reason in order to bring his management expertise to the B-2 program. Kresa knew that Ollie had some strange management habits but felt that he would get the job done.

When Boileau was announced as the temporary head of Grumman, there was certainly no sorrow expressed back in Los Angeles. Many of the Northrop leaders knew that it would be much easier to deal with him at a distance of more than 2,000 miles. Also, when the press release was issued announcing Boileau's new appointment, the release indicated that when the assignment was completed, Boileau would retire from the company. Since Boileau had not been consulted about the announcement, he expressed great concern about his retirement, but eventually he was held to that commitment.

Perhaps Boileau was a skilled manager but he certainly was not a skilled manager of people. Grumman had always considered its people to be its gretest asset and never allowed its executives to treat any employee with outward contempt. That seemed to be the only way Ollie knew how to deal with people, and he created serious morale problems throughout his entire tour of duty. Wherever he went at Grumman he always started his discussions with the reminder that "we bought you" in order to establish his position of superiority. Actually what he established was complete resentment by every Grumman employee.

One of his first actions at the former Grumman headquarters building was to close and lock the men's and ladies' rooms in the executive wing. He had already told every person that still resided in the executive wing that they had one hour to vacate their offices. He said that he would have their property packed and sent to them. Incidentally, he regularly bragged that he was being paid one million dollars to get Grumman straightened out, and he was not going to waste any time doing it.

I have tried to reconcile how closing the bathrooms would improve efficiency one bit. Perhaps he thought that people were coming up to the third floor to use the rest rooms in order to get a glimpse of him, the famous one. Or perhaps he felt that there was too much time being lost by people that were taking care of their physical needs and he wanted to cut down on that time.

Another of his important executive tasks was to inspect every executive office supply stock and as he went through each one, he would throw all of the supplies into the aisles announcing that this was the reason that Grumman was inefficient. There were too many uncontrolled office supplies. As he created this chaos, he sent out a memo to all hands that the entire Bethpage complex was in deplorable condition and he wanted it cleaned up immediately. This was done at the same time that he was trashing the office supply rooms.

Another of his important executive decisions was to direct that all Grumman show cases in the lobbies be emptied of all Grumman products and all of the models were to be packed and shipped to Northrop's West Coast headquarters. A few employees did pack the models but they hid them in the records center in Bethpage. At one point I understand that Ollie ordered the Grumman History Center closed. It was only through the intervention of some persistent employees who talked to their congressman that this order was rescinded.

One employee told me that he was summoned to Ollie's office. When he arrived Ollie went into a tirade about why flowers would not grow in his office. The young man answered that it might have been the language that was being used and all of the shouting in the office all of the time. Ollie grabbed the young man by the collar and escorted him out of the office without ever telling him why he had been summoned.

Ollie of course had the use of a company car and the car was serviced by the Grumman transportation department. Ollie told Cliff Heitzman, head of that department, that he always kept change in the car's center console and he expected that the change would be there when he had the car delivered to him after being serviced. Heitzman joked that every time the car was brought in, he would add a quarter to the change pile. Ollie's reputation had spread so rapidly among the employees that he was usually considered a joke.

Ollie's behavior and reputation was not limited to inside the walls of Grumman. The Human Resources Department found a nice apartment for Ollie and his wife in a gated community in West Islip. He apparently carried on there to the extent that when he left, the management of that facility asked that Grumman not send any other executives there to live.

Unfortunately these actions and several more like them formulated the first impression that Grumman employees got of their new Northrop management. These same employees had not yet recovered from the shock of the sale of Grumman to Northrop and their new Northrop leader, who was soon nick-named "Ollie the Destroyer," was an example of the lives that they had to look forward to in the years ahead. We may never truly understand the negative effect that Ollie Boileau had on these employees. What we do know is that his behavior as a respected executive of their new company was the cause of a great many good employees leaving the company for other opportunities.

Over the years, Grumman, like just about every other large company, had its share of tough managers. I myself worked for several of them and perhaps my own employees put me into the same category. The one thing that was always dominant in the managers and executives of Grumman was a strong belief in the people who made the company what it was. During the short period of time when Ollie Boileau ran Grumman, that respect for the quality and integrity of all employees disappeared. Hopefully the next generation of managers and executives of Northrop Grumman can re-establish the respect and trust that is so important to a harmonious working environment and a successful organization.

Chapter Eleven

Making the Transition Process Work

From the time of that controversial Board meeting at Grumman in January, it took more than two months to finalize all of the formalities of the acquisition. During that time, Jim Roche and Dick Waugh were busy preparing submittals for compliance with the Hart-Scott-Rodino Act of 1976. This law requires that no mergers or acquisitions can be finalized until approval is received from the US Federal Trade Commission and the Department of Justice. These two agencies must determine that the transaction will not adversely affect U.S. commerce under the anti-trust laws.

Roche was handling the inputs to the Federal Trade Commission with Waugh dealing with the submittals to the Department of Justice. Roche later told me that all of the work we had done previously briefing our respective Boards, made that job a lot easier. Approval was received with no difficulty.

When Kent Kresa appointed Jim Roche and me as Co-Chairmen of the transition activities, we realized that our task was not simply to find the quickest way to put the two companies together, but to do it without a dictatorial atmosphere. We never lost sight of the mandate from Kresa to turn hostility into friendship. In the previous months where we had done a good deal of study of the synergies among the two companies, we always worked within an atmosphere of cooperation between like technological experts and leaders. Now with Grumman becoming the acquired company, there was a danger of the atmosphere of cooperation disappearing. Ollie Boileau had already begun his program of intimidation at Grumman, and we knew that we had to try to counter that attitude if we were to be successful in achieving a "best of the best" integration. This meant that we expected to use the techniques, technologies, processes, and procedures from whatever company had shown the best results with their methods.

Throughout this book, you may have noticed little discussion of the level of monetary savings or increases in efficiency that needed to result from the combination of the two companies. Of course those factors were important during early deliberations, but we stayed clear of amplifying their importance until merger or acquisition activities were completed.

Considering the huge investment that Northrop had made to acquire Grumman, the ability to realize financial gains took on new importance. Despite that, we decided not to make the financial issues the focus of our integration efforts. Our theory was that if we put smart people together in small groups with common interests and capabilities, these people would recognize the importance of eliminating redundancies and overlaps in effort. If we gave the project leaders the right motivation, they would automatically produce the changes that would lead to cost savings. Both companies had very positive experiences through their Total Quality Programs where groups of employees got together to solve operational process problems. One over-riding objective that was to guide every project team was the requirement not to take any actions that would jeopardize current program performance. All programs were to move forward as previously planned and key customer representatives were to be kept apprised of all positive progress toward an integrated company.

One example that our process worked was a preliminary directive by the leaders of the Military Aircraft Groups that created self-established financial targets which were much more difficult than we would have dictated. Their self-enforced targets included: a $35 million reduction in staffing and non-allowed costs above what had already been established in their operating plans; a 3% or $30 million reduction in overhead; a $35 million reduction in procurement costs; a $100 million reduction in Gross PP&E; a $12 million reduction in facility costs; and a 15% sales adjusted working capital target which was equivalent to $160 million reduction.

These self imposed targets were an example of how seriously the teams took their assignments. They clearly understood their future was going to be determined by the success of the new company.

When the information was released to the media that Kresa had appointed Jim Roche and me to head the transition team to put the two companies together, Jim Bernstein, the defense industry reporter for Long Island Newsday, made an interesting comment which was kind of representative of how I felt when I got the assignment. He said "the transition leaders will have their work cut out for them. How do two giants get into the same bed without the bed collapsing under them?"

The weight of the task wasn't the thing that bothered me about the assignment. I had worked closely with Roche for nearly a year and during that time we had worked as equals with no concern for who might be in charge. Now the situation had changed. The question now was, "Could we continue to work as unbiased equals with complete objectivity when Northrop, represented by Roche, was clearly the new lead element of this combination?"

That golden handshake that Jim and I had made months ago was the one factor that somewhat relieved my concerns. My only objective for my integration effort was to do the best job I could to insure that the surviving company was a success both financially and operationally. If this goal was accomplished, it would be the best gift that I could leave for the Grumman employees who remained part of the new Northrop Grumman.

I was not yet 60 years old, but I had pledged to Roche and Kresa that I would retire when the merger was completed. There were no personal goals involved here and would not be during the months ahead. I felt that it was time to hand the baton to the next generation who were likely younger and better able to carry the company well into the future with new and fresh ideas. I believe that it was this factor and the complete respect that Jim and I had developed for each other that allowed us to achieve our objective without collapsing the bed.

One of the strengths we agreed was a contributor to the 2+2=5 concept was the existence of many "key personnel" in both organizations. These were people who had established themselves as experts in their respective fields or had become critical to the management of the on-going programs. One aspect of failed acquisitions that has filled the history books is the loss of key personnel after an acquisition or merger takes place. Every company has several key people involved in daily program activities that would seriously hurt those programs if they left the company. One objective that Jim and I established early in the transition program was to attempt to identify these key people. Key personnel are not always in significant management positions. They are often people that are waiting in the wings to rise in the company because they have demonstrated outstanding technical or job capabilities but have not yet attained a recognizable management position. During the integration studies and briefings, we had established a plan to make note of these people because they would likely be the future backbone of the new company. It is sometimes not sufficient to depend on existing management to come forward to identify key personnel since these same people are often considered a threat to their existing managers. In the process of working with each of the integration groups, it was not difficult to determine who the people were who were the driving forces behind their specific functions.

We had already defined twenty seven areas that needed further definition including the key leaders from each company representing these areas. Our first task was to appoint two facilitators who would concentrate full time insuring the transition project teams were moving forward. I appointed Ray Duffy, Grummans Director of Strategic Planning and Roche appointed Al Meyers, Northorp's Vice

President, Business Strategy as our lead staff for the transition process. Both of these leaders were forward thinkers who knew the inner workings of their respective companies. Both were also "no nonsense" guys who we knew would keep the project teams on track while Roche and I concentrated on our assigned transition tasks. We also needed to insure that the findings of the individual teams were reviewed and quickly brought before the Corporate Policy Council and eventually signed off by Kent Kresa. Our method was to keep pressure on everyone involved on the project teams to work to a schedule that would complete all of their work by the end of 1994, less than nine months from the start of the deliberations.

A briefing room was set up at the Century City Corporate Headquarters where the activities of each project team were posted and kept current. All of the project team leaders from both companies were brought to Los Angeles and thoroughly briefed on the transition process and our schedule. Jim and I would attend some of the more significant project team meetings when the team was about to come to significant conclusions or perhaps needed more guidance. We made it clear that we would look favorably on the recommendations for eliminating unnecessary or outdated procedures. Overall the intent was to improve the efficiency of the new company to better its competitive capability.

To insure that we set the correct example, Roche and I took leadership of three areas that we had already been studying. We became the leaders of three teams including developing the new corporate organization and structure; achieving quick successes; and insuring that the communications within and between transition project teams was effective. We knew we could post early successes in these categories since the subject matter was a large part of our previous year-long efforts.

My research had shown that one of the most important factors contributing to the success of an integration effort is the effectiveness of communications with the employees. I knew that much of the bitterness that resided within Grumman was caused by the required secretive nature of the activities of the previous months. Employees knew that something was in the wind, but we could not communicate to them exactly what we were up to. To reduce the impact of previous incomplete communications our first action after starting to plan the transition program, was to publish regular "transition updates" to let everyone know exactly what progress (or lack of it) was taking place. The first "transition update" was released on April 22, 1994 outlining our communication objectives and providing a Northrop Grumman Information Line phone number. Those with questions about on-going procedures could call this hot line and receive the latest information available.

Following shortly after the first update were others that described the procedures for transition studies and implementation, the new corporate organization, and the use of video conferencing to speed communications. Also included was an outline and definition of each of the transition project teams that had been established, including the leaders from both companies. There were 27 project teams established covering the following areas:

Employment and Development

Benefits

Corporate Office Re-design

Facilities

Policy and Procedures

Information Systems and Services

Customer Relations

Quick Successes

2+2=5 Project

Total Quality Integration

Overall Organizational Structure

Manufacturing Operations

Procurement

Legal

Advanced Development and Planning Non-Traditional

Advanced Development Planning and Review

Advanced Development and Technology Base

Communications

Consultants and Advisors

Public Affairs and State Relations

Aircraft Systems Business Strategy

Commercial Aerostructures Business Strategy

International

Investor Relations

Financial Management and Control Practices

Superior Financial Performance

Electronics and Systems Integration Business Strategy

Each Project team consisted of one leader from each company and however many other subject experts were considered necessary. We didn't limit the number of people involved on each team, we considered it most important to get the expert opinions from both companies and make everyone feel that there was a participative environment in existence. Each team was also represented by an executive member of the Corporate Policy Council who would provide guidance, eventually taking the findings to the council for review and approval.

One of our first acts was to define the procedures to be used to insure that the results and recommendations of each Project Team are quickly implemented. The findings of each Project team were to be documented and presented to the Corporate Policy Council. This Council consisted of the senior executives of Northrop Grumman including Roche and me. The intent was to quickly modify or approve the recommendations and forward them to Kent Kresa for rapid approval and implementation. Kresa had promised to provide a decision on every project team recommendation within 24 hours of receiving it. He kept that promise throughout the transition process.

It is interesting to note that shortly after the new Corporate structure was announced, Kresa continued his strategy of a friendly combination by naming two Grumman executives to fill key positions in the new organization. Gerald Sandler was named to head the new Data Systems and Services Division and John Harrison was named to head the Electronics and Systems Integration Division. Both of these appointments were somewhat of a surprise to me since I knew that Kresa's long range strategic plan was to re-build the company around these two Divisions. In retrospect however, as Kresa's strategy began to develop through additional acquisitions, both of these men left the company.

During our previous discussions concerning a merger, we naturally discussed several issues that were not central to the synergies or financial opportunities. One such subject related to the name of the resulting company. We both wanted to keep each company's identity intact. For me, it was the feeling that there was a strong heritage associated with the Grumman name in both aircraft design and space exploration. Roche was a history buff and also felt strongly about the Northrop heritage.

We had tentatively agreed that Northrop Grumman sounded better than Grumman Northrop. It simply rolled off the tongue more easily. It really was not our decision to make, but we were prepared to put that recommendation forward to both CEO's if the merger was completed. When the merger opportunity died and was overtaken by the acquisition of Grumman by Northrop, it was now still our mutual recommendation but the decision was now solely in the hands of Northrop. Roche carried the recommendation to Kresa and apparently sold him on the idea. The Grumman name was preserved.

During our deliberations on this issue we reviewed many previous acquisitions that had been made throughout industry and found that in most cases the identity of the acquired company disappeared either immediately after the acquisition or within a relatively short time later. Kresa's approval of the Northrop Grumman name was an extension of his belief that hostile takeovers do not have to result in hostile actions. Retaining the Grumman name reflected his approach to accomplishing a smooth transition and I believe that Roche pushed hard on this issue to retain it.

We announced that our goal was to have all of the project team work completed and reviewed so they could be fully implemented and operational by December 31, 1994.

There were 46 transition updates issued, many containing the findings of several project teams. After the first update was issued on April 22, 1994, significant issues were defined in other updates including the definition of the new corporate organization on May 3; Division management structure announced on June 8; Corporate strategy changes announced on June 9; Stock transfer procedures announced on June 15; new benefits announced on July 8; Electronics Division organization announced on Aug 15; Vought acquisition procedures announced on Aug 18; Data Systems organization announced on Sept 9; Benefits changes announced on Sept.26; and Commercial Aircraft Division announced on Oct 4. These were only a few of the significant announcements issued through the transition updates.

All transition objectives were completed on time. The 46th issue of the "Transition Update" was released on December 20, 1994, and the Merger Line was disconnected on December 23, 1994, having received more than 7,000 calls since its inception. The entire transition program was completed within nine months from its start in April 1994.

I believe that the use of employee and management teams, to examine each of the selected areas, was one element of our approach to integration that paid dividends. It quickly put key members of both companies together in a cooperative work environment with clearly defined goals and schedules. This technique was also partially responsible for overcoming the damage that Boileau had done to Grumman morale during his reign as temporary head of Grumman.

Chapter Twelve

A Period of Misunderstanding

During my tenure as co-chair of the transition team, I had the opportunity to spend several months at the former Grumman headquarters facility in Bethpage. I was alternating my time between New York and Los Angeles. My transition team activities allowed me to talk to hundreds of former Grumman employees who used the opportunity to vent some of their frustrations and concerns. One fact quickly became obvious to me during this period. The issues related to Grumman's financial and business situation prior to the takeover by Northrop were clearly misunderstood by the majority of those with whom I spoke. There was a serious resentment toward Grumman's executive management for acting so rapidly during those last few months. Most were unaware that we had been working for more than two years, trying to come up with some solution that would permit the company to continue to go it alone.

It's not a traditional management policy, certainly not at Grumman, to stand before the employees and tell them the company is in serious financial difficulty. The accepted route is to work hard to correct that situation quietly so as not to spread concern or even fear among the work force. From the time that Renso Caporali took over leadership of Grumman in 1990, he had worked tirelessly to fix the problems that had been created by decisions made decades earlier. He had improved the company's value by taking those actions necessary to increase the stock price from its low of $13 per share up to $43. The company's debt had been reduced to nearly zero. Caporali achieved a reduction in working capital of more than $400 million. Factory floor space was reduced by 30%, manufacturing labor rates were significantly reduced and product costs were brought down by 16%. Restructuring charges of $85 million were offset by over $600 million in cost savings. BUT! The premature end of the F-14 program was a blow that Grumman was unable to survive. Despite the win on the JSTARS program, it was not enough to fix the problem. As a matter of fact the JSTARS program required an additional investment.

During the deliberations and studies to integrate the two companies, it was discovered that the Grumman pension program could possibly have been under funded. This would have presented an additional financial burden to Grumman which, if not corrected, could have affected the pensions of thousands of former Grumman employees. Fortunately when the acquisition was completed, Northrop Grumman management made the decision to merge the Grumman pension program with the Northrop program, essentially solving the funding problem.

At the time of the Government announced "last supper," and later with the cancellation of the F-14 program, every member of Grumman's executive staff recognized that something had to be done and done fast or we would be left behind. Much of the industry was reacting to the Government's warning and was already starting to consolidate. As a result of our internal studies, the difficult decision had already been made that Grumman's future would not include remaining a major aircraft builder. When Caporali approved the company's new strategic statement redirecting its operations away from aircraft manufacturing he confided to me that this was the most difficult decision he ever had to make, but it was a move that was clearly necessary for any sort of company survival.

We went down the path of trying to acquire other companies that had similar core capabilities, but our financial situation would not allow us to be competitive in those efforts. We investigated merger possibilities with other systems oriented companies, but could not generate enough interest to complete any of those transactions. The best possible outcome as a result of these attempts was to move toward a friendly merger. This path would likely permit much of the company to remain intact. A merger would also allow some of Grumman's management to remain in positions to have a say in future events. Change would still be necessary but it might be less dramatic through a merger. That was the path that we selected.

As one who was part of nearly every event of the last two years of Grumman's existence, I believe I can state rather conclusively that there was not one member of the Grumman executive team that wanted the company to take this route. Bob Myers, Grumman's President continued to state that he would like to try and go it alone. Renso Caporali had been appointed Grumman's CEO only three years earlier. He had worked hard to bring Grumman though its financial crisis, and he certainly did not want to have his career marked by the company's disappearance. Bob Anderson, Grumman's CFO was a relative newcomer to the company, but he had made several significant financial changes that were just now starting to have a positive effect. He certainly wanted to take more time to see the true effects of his efforts. BUT! These executives, like the rest of the corporate executive team also knew what cards were on the table and we did not hold a winning hand. Through all of the dozens of discussions that Bob Denien, Dick Anderson and I had with Northrop, there was never a day that we did not wish for some miracle to happen to change our direction, but that miracle never happened.

Recognizing the bitterness among the Grumman employees, Chairman Caporali released a letter to all employees through the Grumman World publication that attempted to explain the need for secrecy. The contents of that letter were presented earlier in this book.Although this letter showed good intentions, it did not go very far toward soothing employee tensions.

One of the first rumors that spread through the organization was that Grumman's top management had made significant financial gains from the takeover. Let me clear up that point. Every Grumman stock holder that held company stock at the conclusion of the takeover received a significant capital gain from the final transaction. This was not limited to Grumman management. There were a few of the top executives that were, years earlier granted a "golden parachute." This was common practice among all large companies to insure that these executives would act in the best interest of the shareholders in any future negotiations as part of a change in ownership. As one who received this status, I can speak with experience on this matter. This program called for each recipient to receive 2.99 times their annual salary in case of a change of ownership. When the Northrop sale was completed, those of us who held this benefit were told by the Company's outside accounting firm, that the IRS was going to consider this award a windfall profit and the award would be taxed so high that we would receive nothing in the end. That indeed was the case so that the golden parachute was worthless in this case and no financial reward was ever realized by any executive as a result.

Another inaccurate rumor that was circulated indicated that Grumman's restricted stock program had a "change of ownership" clause that would double the value of the stock in case of a takeover. As one who had been awarded restricted stock, I can attest to the fact that this was not true. Restricted stock was surrendered at the current sale price. I have not been able to find anyone who has heard of or who received this price doubling. The rumor was just that, a rumor. It is probably typical of the unsettling discussions that were taking place at the time of the sale. It all seemed to happen so fast that everyone was making up their own stories to blame management for the events of the final days.

Throughout the entire year of discussions with Northrop management, both Grumman and Northrop personnel involved in the discussions took great care to establish an atmosphere of trust and mutual respect. We felt it was important to lay a foundation for the future merger that was free of any concern for individual maneuvering for position or organizational protection. The golden handshake that Jim Roche and I made early in the game was the beginning of this atmosphere of trust.

When the activities of the early months of 1994 turned our peaceful discussion into a hostile takeover, Kent Kresa asked us both to do everything in our power to maintain the atmosphere of friendship that we had established. He felt that a hostile takeover attitude needed to be left in the board rooms of the two companies. The success of the resulting company was going to be based on actions that were to be taken in the months to come. Hostility, according to Kresa was to be left behind in favor of a businesslike approach to putting the two companies together. Unfortunately Kresa's appointment of Boileau as temporary head of Grumman operations was a serious setback to his "peaceful integration" strategy.

But there were some other rough edges to this strategy. Perhaps not everyone bought in to the concept. A merger would have resulted in detailed discussions of how the two entities would be put together, who the leaders would be, how the organization would develop and most importantly, what was needed to maintain customer satisfaction during the transition period. Now that Northrop was the buyer, that all changed. The challenge now was to bring Grumman into the Northrop family in the most effective manner. It was clearly the job of Jim and I to find ways to overcome these strategy weaknesses.

Despite all of the concerns held by Grumman employees and their appalling treatment by Boileau, I have to applaud them here for the professional manner in which they handled and participated in all of the transition activities that took place during 1994. Most of the key people that were picked to participate in the transition team efforts knew that their efforts would go a long way in defining the future success of the new company. They also knew that their efforts during the transition period would help define their individual capability to be part of that future. I will always be proud of the way the Grumman employees performed during those difficult days.

Chapter Thirteen

Another Government About Face

The acquisition of Grumman by Northrop was never considered to be the end game for the resulting company. Even during Grumman's Project X studies, it was concluded that additional expansion would be needed subsequent to a merger. Kent Kresa was a strategically oriented executive and he knew that this latest combination was only the beginning of building a company that could rival Boeing and Lockheed. During the end of my tour a co-chairman of the transition team, I was asked to participate in the preparation of the company's next strategic plan. Kresa made it clear to the team preparing this plan that his vision was to continue to expand the company through acquisitions. I will deal with more specifics of this plan later in this book, but at this point I want to once again point out the difficulties of running a company that derives most of its revenue from the US Government.

In December 1996, many in the industry were shocked by Boeing's purchase of McDonnell Douglas Corp for $14 Billion. Grumman management was particularly surprised since less than two years earlier Boeing showed no interest in expanding. Raytheon, seemingly out of nowhere, followed close behind Boeing with the purchase of the defense businesses of Hughes Electronics Corp. and Texas Instruments. These two purchases amounted to about $12.5 billion. It was clear now that Northrop Grumman was again in a position of being unable to compete in the same league as the now newly formed big three, Boeing, Lockheed Martin and Raytheon.

Kresa and Norm Augustine, CEO of Lockheed Martin, decided to get together and determine the best approach to remaining competitive with the other more powerful defense companies. After an intense series of discussions, Lockheed Martin announced on July 3, 1997 that it planned to acquire Northrop Grumman for $8.3 billion.. The two CEO's concluded that this combination would create a balanced company that would present a challenge to the huge, powerful companies created by both Boeing and Raytheon. It also seemed that this was a logical conclusion to the several year consolidations that were directed by the defense department at the "last supper" meeting that took place previously. After all, it was that "last supper" meeting that started Grumman on its way to combining with Northrop.

Secretary of defense Bill Perry was leaving his post to the newly appointed Senator William Cohen. At the confirmation hearing for Cohen, he indicated that he was concerned about the dwindling competition among the large defense companies. Cohen's concern at this time seemed odd since the consolidation movements that had already occurred were dictated by a Defense Department led by many of the same people. At the same time the Justice Department was installing a new antitrust chief named Joel Klein. Klein had made it clear that when dealing with defense issues, his office would do everything in its power to protect competition. WOW! All of the sudden another top official is now concerned about competition. It was almost immediately after the Klein statement that Lockheed Martin announced the purchase of Northrop Grumman. The words of both Klein and Cohen might have been a signal of trouble for the Lockheed Martin purchase of Northrop Grumman, but if any signal was given, it was not received by either company. During merger discussions, both companies had discussed possible combinations with their major military customers and found no real objection. Surely the military leaders would be consulted about this merger.

In September of 1997, Navy brass sent a report to the Pentagon's merger review chief indicating its full support for a merger of these two companies. The report indicated that Lockheed Martin had little experience building Navy aircraft and the combination with Northrop Grumman would offer good competition to Boeing for the upcoming Joint Strike Fighter. The Navy also felt good about a merger that might keep Grumman's Navy aircraft design capability intact.

Shortly after the Navy endorsement of the deal, the Air Force also came to the conclusion that the Lockheed Martin deal with Northrop Grumman would not reduce competition in military aircraft. There had also been rumors that some Air Force brass was concerned that if Lockheed didn't survive, they would be faced with a Boeing monopoly. The CEO's of both Northrop Grumman and Lockheed Martin felt confident that with the full endorsement of both miliitary service customers, approval would be assured.

Unfortunately the military services apparently did not have a primary role in the decision process for these types of mergers. They only played an advisory role in the process. The final decisions are made by the Secretary of Defense where the entire advisory staff consists of civilian employees, most of whom have no military experience. This now starts to look exactly like the decision that drove Grumman out of the aircraft business where the military brass wanted the Grumman product but the civilian advisors wanted another product. That decision drove Grumman out of the airplane building business and caused it to seek a partnership with Northrop.

Here we find ourselves a few years later in the same quagmire of events. Changes were taking place throughout the government establishment and also within Lockheed Martin. Norm Augustine was stepping down as CEO of Lockheed

Martin, being replaced by Vance Coffman. Augustine was perhaps one of the most skilled of the defense leaders when it came to working his way through the defense establishment. Coffman was far less experienced in that arena.

Changes were also being made at the Justice Department with Klein taking over as antitrust chief. Neither Lockheed Martin nor Northrop Grumman had much experience dealing with the Justice department on issues like this. All previous merger reviews were conducted largely by the U.S. Federal Trade Commission.

Changes were also taking place in the Pentagon where officials who had participated in previous merger reviews were leaving. The post of Pentagon Acquisition Chief was being filled by Jacques Gansler, who was an engineer with a doctorate in economics. Gansler had previously made his position known that the best efficiency would be achieved by attracting more companies into the defense marketplace. Shortly after his appointment to his new position, Gansler found a new objection to industrial consolidation, stating that vertical integration resulting from mergers would cause the big companies to select suppliers from their own stable of companies, rather than looking outside for the best fit of suppliers. When the final decision was handed down blocking the Lockheed merger with Northrop Grumman, Gansler's vertical integration argument was used as the major factor.

There is another factor that is rarely discussed regarding this shocking Government change in direction. Raytheon was rumored to have mounted a massive campaign in objection to the Lockheed Martin, Northrop Grumman merger. Raytheon officials denied that rumor but it was revealed that of the 200 boxes of data that were gathered by the various reviewing agencies, 140 of those boxes were supplied by Raytheon. The main argument that Raytheon used was the same argument posed by Gansler. They maintained that Lockheed Martin would deal at arm's length when selecting subcontractors in favor of its own units over those of outsiders.

When Lockheed Martin management heard of the vertical integration argument, they made a vigorous appeal, presenting several examples that indicated that vertical integration was not a problem. At the conclusion of their presentation, they felt confident that their appeal would be effective, especially since their military customers were supportive of the combination.

Both Lockheed Martin and Northrop Grumman executives were so confident of a positive decision that Northrop Grumman issued a transition notice clarifying how the names of the two companies would be integrated. The Corporate name would be Lockheed Martin and the heritage names of the Northrop Grumman divisions would remain with those divisions. This transition notice was distributed on

February 26, 1998 and projected that the integration of the companies would be completed within three months.

On March 4, executives from Lockheed Martin and Northrop Grumman were invited to a meeting in Washington but were not given an agenda. Norm Augustine noted to the group that this meeting was in a pentagon conference room adjacent to the room where the "last supper' was held a few years ago. For more than an hour, these executives listened with shock as they were told that the government was about to oppose the merger. Augustine was quoted as stating that over the course of his career, he had attended thousands of meeting at the Pentagon and this was the by far the worse meeting he had ever attended.

Days after this meeting, the Pentagon endorsed the Justice Department's suit to block the deal. This was the first time in history that either of these agencies had taken the position to stop a major defense industry acquisition. While announcing their decision, Attorney General Janet Reno called the merger anticompetitive and indicated that it threatened the military. She further stated: "we want to ensure that any defense merger protects our soldier's lives."

At this point I must interject my personal opinion about these events. During the course of my career at Grumman, I personally dealt with some of the principle decision makers in this case when they served in lesser jobs. Bill Perry, who was stepping down as Defense Secretary had worked directly with me during our early Project X studies under contract with Grumman. Perry was an intelligent individual who was very knowledgeable about defense affairs and familiar with the people and procedures of both Lockheed Martin and Northrop Grumman. I do not believe that he would support a second rate excuse like vertical integration. I had several meetings with Ganzler when he was an under secretary encouraging companies to consider cost as a design factor for their aircraft designs. I always considered him a smart guy, but his career as a bureaucrat also made him an expert at taking orders from above. I cannot rationalize that these same people could seize upon such a mundane argument as vertical integration or damaging the military to support what was an obviously political decision, not based on any common sense business considerations. It sounded to me like a political decision was made at a very high level that was simply echoed by the supposed decision maker bureaucrats at the lower levels.

It's ironic that the exact same technique was used when the military was overruled by the bureaucrats when deciding to cancel the Grumman F-14 in favor of the McDonnell F-18. The cast of characters was different, but the procedure was the same and the results once again did not favor the Grumman team.

When Did the Procurement Process Change?

As I look back over the last thirty years, I often ask myself, when did the military procurement process change? When did civilian politicians get the level of power that they make significant military decisions without high level military input? For most of my career the functions of the various elements of Government had clearly defined roles in the procurement process. Of course, as I have described in the few actual political stories I have included, politics has always played a role in the budgetary process for the procurement of military weapon systems. But the roles and missions of the various government agencies were always fairly well defined. Somewhere along the way things changed and I'm not quite sure exactly when that happened.

To me, the most startling example happened as I was doing research for this book. There was a major military operation going on in a troubled area of the world. American soldiers were involved in a serious combat situation. All television stations were covering this operation with their 24/7 coverage and imbedded reporters. The television screen panned to the White House situation room where real time decisions were being made. Most shocking to me was the complete absence of any member of the gathered tribunal that was wearing a military uniform. Decisions were being transmitted to combat strategists by politicians and civilian staff with no military experience or knowledge." Where were the Joint Chiefs" I asked myself. Perhaps they were in the room but not panned by the cameras. If so, they should have been at the right hand of the President providing him information based on their years of experience in such military situations. This, to me, was a startling example of how things have changed in Washington and how decisions previously made by career military personnel are now being made by inexperienced and possibly incompetent civilians.

For as long as I can remember, the annual budget process defined the extent of the procurement budget for each of the military services. The services would make requests for new programs as part of that budget process. Some requests would be approved and others would be deferred or rejected. For the most part military needs were left to the military commanders and budget decisions were left to congress. It wasn't always that simple but in principal it worked well.

If new programs were approved, the service would send out invitations to bid (RFP's) to industry. Interested companies would respond with their designs and prices. The service procurement leaders would evaluate each proposal and select the winning design. That was it. Perhaps I've over simplified the process but that was how it worked. Of course, the companies that had made the correct decisions about their research were better prepared to submit leading edge designs than those who were less technically qualified. Oh, there were sometimes protests, but they were rare and rarely succeeded.

As technology advanced and weapon systems became more complex, the need for companies to invest to keep up became a differentiator among qualified companies. Defense companies started to carve out their specialty areas so as to reduce their investments. Some companies concentrated on airframe design while others specialized in electronics integration. This caused large defense companies to create teams to compete on major programs.

As time progressed and weapons became extremely complex, the government started requiring companies to make enormous investments in both capital and technology. This is when the defense business got risky and competition for new programs became questionable. Companies that were asked to make enormous investments were asking in return for some security that the quantities to be procured would be guaranteed. Of course the federal budget process would not permit those types of guarantees beyond a given fiscal year, so defense companies began to put more emphasis on the contract language that would protect their financial investments. Some services were fairly cooperative in this regard and others were not. The contracting process became somewhat hostile. Since the beginning of weapons procurement history, funding for design and development was normally paid by the government as part of the contractual agreements. Because of the high risk nature of development, payments were normally made on a cost reimbursement basis meaning that contractors were paid for all costs plus a fee. This form of contracting is what gave the defense industry the reputation for being a low risk industry.

Then things started to change as the government started to tighten the strangle hold on companies that had won major contracts. The services started demanding that defense companies provide fixed prices even for development. This changed the financial posture of every defense company because it was a virtual guarantee that they would lose money on development contracts. On advanced technology products, it is absolutely impossible to adequately estimate the cost of invention. There are too many unknowns and Murphy's Law always comes into effect. If something can go wrong, it will go wrong. To counter this trend toward fixed priced development contracts, defense companies had to amortize their development losses over the life of the production program for those products. This presented even greater risk since most production quantity predictions by the government were always overstated. The annual congressional budget review process almost always made reductions in procurement quantities to help reduce budgetary overages.

In the 1980's when Ronald Reagan took office, he was a supporter of expanded military spending and during that period all hell broke loose. The "Ill wind" scandals that I previously described created such a stir throughout Washington that literally every agency that was, in any way, involved in weapons procurement started modifying their procurement procedures, making it even more difficult to do profitable business in military procurement. I believe that this is the benchmark period when the entire defense industry began to unravel.

Politics now found its way into nearly every aspect of the military procurement process. Rather than concentrating its efforts on solving some of the serious problems of the country, congress would hold extensive hearings on why an ashtray placed in an aircraft cost the government $600 or why the cost of a hammer was $800. I personally testified at the ash tray hearings. These hearings took weeks of testimony and wasted thousands of hours of people's time. Every defense company was on 24 hour call to respond as requested to committee questions on issues such as the $600 ashtray. Hour after hour of proof was provided that the cost of these non-critical items was driven by the government's own procurement policies, but the hearing became more of a witch hunt where even the identity of the witch became blurred.

As government procedures became more complicated, a bigger government bureaucracy was developed to monitor and control these procedures. Now, complicated and often unreasonable procedures were job savers for government employees so the growth in government continued and still continues today.

So, is it a surprise to us that this bureaucratic nightmare has affected every Grumman and Northrop Grumman employee? It was a shocking surprise back in 1991 when the Secretary of Defense called the heads of every large defense firm to Washington and informed them that the future would not support their existence and they were told to take necessary action to reduce the size of the defense industrial base by 50%. This set off a consolidation effort that affected the lives of millions of Americans who had built their careers in the defense industry.

Should it have been a surprise in 1992 when, despite the Navy brass endorsing the continuation of the F-14 program, the civilian leaders ruled against that recommendation in favor of the yet to be developed F-18. Sounds like politics again ruled over the military.

Extending history still further, following the direction given by government leaders, Boeing bought McDonald Douglas in 1996 for $14 billion with no government interference. Shortly after that Raytheon bought Hughes and Texas Instruments for about $12billion. Again there was no government interference. But in 1997 when Northrop Grumman agreed to be purchased by Lockheed Martin for approximately $8.3 billion, the government said NO! Despite both the Air Force and Navy expressing approval of the acquisition, career government civilian employees maintained that this merger would damage the competitive environment at the subcontracting level. This process of permitting civilian employees to overrule the military experts took Northrop Grumman from being part of the country's largest defense firm if combined with Lockheed Martin, to being the fourth largest company. Doesn't seem quite fair does it? A conspiracy theorist might be tempted to ask if there might not be someone highly placed within the government that simply does not want a company with a Grumman name to survive.

Chapter Fourteen

Northrop Grumman Growth History

Apparently the trials and tribulations of the Grumman acquisition in 1994 and the failed attempt to combine with Lockheed Martin in 1997 gave Northrop Grumman management new motivation and a few new tricks to continue to grow the company. Since the Grumman purchase in 1994, Northrop Grumman has made 25 additional aquisitions to grow the company's employment to more than 120,000 people. The acquisition strategy directed by CEO Kent Kresa has been based on his stated strategic direction to take the company into a leadership position not only in its core business of electronic integration, and aircraft system development, but to advance the company as the leader in information technology related to cyber warfare and electronic surveillance. Through an aggressive acquisition strategy which included several hostile takeovers and adding more than 10 information oriented companies, Kresa has achieved his objective. He indicated to me in a recent interview, that hostile beginnings almost always become non-hostile operations after the acquisition. He attributes this to a properly planned and implemented transition program. Since the acquisition of Grumman in

1994, Northrop Grumman has made the following additional acquisitions.

Westinghouse Defense Electronics..1996

Logicon..1997

Teledyne Ryan Aeronautics..1999

Litton Industries..2001

Newport News Shipbuilding..2001

TRW..2002

Inter-National Research Institute..1998

California Microwave Systems..1999

Data Procurent Corp..1999

Navia Aviation AS..2000

Comptek Research Inc..2000

Federal Data Corp..2000

Sterling Software Inc..2000

Aerojet General Corp. Electronics & Info Systems Div..2001

Fibersense Technology Corp..2002

XonTech..2003

LLigen Simulation T echnologies..2003

Confluent..2005

Integic Corp..2005

Essex Corp..2007

Xinetics..2007

Scaled Composites..2007

3001 International..2008

M5 Networks Security..2012

Quantas Defense Services..2014

The going has not always been smooth for the company but in terms of shareholder value, Northrop Grumman has been a fine investment for shareholders as shown in the following normalized chart.

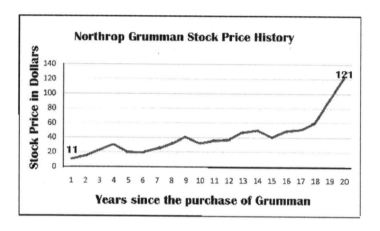

At the end of the first year of operation after the Grumman purchase the company's stock value fell to around $11 dollars per share. Since that time the value has increased about 50% per year to the point where in 2014 the stock price was at more than $121 dollars and I believe that there was a stock split along the way. Another way to express this growth would be that the value of Northrop Grumman stock has increased by a factor of ten times over a period of twenty years.

Chapter Fifteen

Some Could Ask "So What"

A friend of mine who was also a long term Grummanite and is now a successful author, Wyman "Sandy" Jones was talking with me recently as I was researching for this book. As an experienced author Sandy knows the right questions to ask in terms of what makes a book interesting. He said, "after you do all of this research and lay out all of the true facts to your readers, someone might read all of your information and at the end ask, so what?"

The more I thought about Sandy's statement, the more interesting it became. I certainly don't believe that reading this book will change anyone's life significantly. It has been more than twenty years since the events took place that I describe in this book. Many of the actual players are no longer with us. Many who were around during those times may not remember what happened or don't care. Some may chose not to remember. My interest was simply to put in place the events of the 1990's to insure their proper place in history, and to provide enough information for the readers to learn from past experiences.

I spent 33 years, 95% of my career, working for Grumman. They were years that I choose to remember, not forget. Like thousands of other Grumman employees, my career at Grumman helped pay for the food I fed my family. It helped send my children to college. It helped me afford to buy my home and it helped keep me healthy enough so that at the age of 78, I still have enough left inside me to do the work necessary to write this book. I am proud of my years at Grumman and I want to express that pride by documenting the final chapter in the history of this great company.

When I was a young child, I might not have understood why I had to study the history of events that had occurred hundreds of years ago. Over the course of several decades, world events continued to remind me why it was important during those early years to understand the meaning of our country's founders, their principals, and their motivations. Nearly every year, someone in this country tries to alter the basic principals upon which this country was founded. Had I not been taught the basic truths many years ago, I might not appreciate how important they are today toward holding the fiber of our country together. Oh, I'm not trying to say that the events of this book have that degree of importance, they certainly do not. But for the thousands of people who dedicated a large part of their life giving their best to this company, I believe that they should know exactly how the history of the company ended. For those still employed, this book might help them stay focused on those events that may cause a similar fate to happen again.

For thousands of people, the acquisition of Grumman by Northrop was not the end of a career, but the beginning of a new one. Perhaps many more thousands of people ended their career when the change was made. For both of these groups, I believe it is important to know just how important their contributions were and still are toward achieving individual and corporate success. I want the employees of today to better understand the difficulties of trying to manage a big company in today's new liberal society where achievement and creativeness are giving way to individual wants and needs. I encourage all employees to try to keep up to date with world events that will drive the success of their company in the near future.

During the early 70's and 80's, when the defense business was booming, none of us really understood or could have expected that a change in national political priorities would drive a flourishing healthy company to its knees in a few short months. But, it happened and there was not one thing that Grumman management could have done differently to prevent that tragedy. The future of Grumman was altered by one stroke of a pen of one government official.

As I look at the events of the 2014 era and try to project beyond this period, there is little doubt in my mind that the industrial consolidation events of the 1990's will be repeated and possibly very soon. Because our national priorities are changing so rapidly with rising national debt and increased emphasis on improving social programs, the defense industry will soon again have to shrink to the size of its supporting federal budget. There is little room left in the top tier of that industry for more consolidation so it will likely take place at the next lower levels. That means that the larger companies will be expected to take on many of these smaller ones to accomplish this consolidation.

Recognizing these possibilities, every American company is going to have to get the maximum productivity from every element of its organization. This will require that every member of every company will be expected to do their part toward achieving this efficiency, working harder and smarter. The days of expecting a salary increase because a year has passed since the last one, are gone forever. Now, salary increases will be based on increased value to the company, which means that upward mobility of employees will require individual productivity and creativeness while national priorities tend to move toward complacency.

Grumman was one of the last truly paternalistic companies; hierarchical in management structure but employee-focused in culture with generously funded benefits programs. These programs were funded by our customers because in return they received products of exceptional quality. Government customers today no longer permit that attitude. In many sectors of our government, big business is considered evil. Today we live in an entrepreneurial economy driven by global forces and relentless competition coupled with a shrinking level of customer affordability. A whole new paradigm is now required for a large company to survive. This new paradigm will require a completely new set of relationships between employers and employees

So! That's kind of the "so what" of this book, an attempt to show that it is the responsibility of every employee to do as much as possible when times are good and to help their employers build the strength to survive when times are bad. History has always been our ultimate teacher. The best learning comes from understanding the successes and mistakes of the past and applying this learning to mold the events of the future.

Loyalty - A Two-way Street

Those in my age group remember the times when company loyalty was a two-way proposition. We were loyal and dedicated to our employers because they had programs and attitudes that showed their loyalty to us. Grumman was a sterling example of that situation. For decades Grumman would do anything within its power to prevent having to downsize its work force. People who were hired to work at Grumman were encouraged to adopt the attitude that this was not a job, but a career. It was the standard expectation that a job at Grumman would last as long as an employee wanted it to last, provided of course that job performance was consistent. Through its entire existence, Grumman management never felt the threat of its employees wanting a union to represent them. There was no need for third party representation. The company had an open door policy that worked. Grumman employees were part of a family and they felt an obligation to do as much as possible to contribute to the health of that family.

There never seemed to be a threat of the company taking away benefits or reducing salaries. The only serious question that arose every year was if the company would give both a Thanksgiving and Christmas bonus, or if the Christmas turkeys would be larger that year. Nearly every year the company would make some small improvement in one or another of its benefits. The company took care of the health insurance of all employees, it provided improvements in its vacation policies, it established a matching investment plan and many more benefit improvement programs. These were the things that showed the loyalty of the company toward every employee.

Without demanding it, these are also the things that inspired all employees to honor their loyalty to the company. If a problem arose on a program or a proposal or if a schedule commitment was in danger of not being met, Grumman people would often work around the clock, without compensation, to solve the problem.

This commitment of company to employee and employee to company is what set Grumman apart from many of its competitors and our customers knew it and applauded it.

When the Apollo program was concluded, Grumman, for the first time in its history, was faced with the situation of ending the jobs of thousands of its loyal employees. Management struggled with ways to avoid this calamity, but there was no avoiding the reduction. The experience was traumatic to thousands of employees who had bet their careers on Grumman.

This is probably the point in Grumman's history when employees felt that the company's loyalty to them was in question. Consequently their loyalty to the company would also follow suit. It wasn't that it was anyone's fault. It was just an event of the times. The loss of a massive program such as the Lunar Module required that the company tighten its belt for the first time in its history. It was a matter of survival. But none the less, the issue of corporate loyalty, in the minds of the employees, was no longer a factor. It was gone.

It wasn't only Grumman that suffered this traumatic experience. Nearly every large company was faced with the same dilemma. Young people were not signing on for the long haul and many were simply taking one job as a stepping stone for the next one. This created a situation where corporate managers needed to develop new management techniques to try to insure upward mobility as an incentive for career planning for employees, or at least for those who were interested and capable of moving up.

Today, more than a decade after the turn of the century, the responsibilities of companies toward their employees and employees toward their companies is still being defined. Unfortunately we are also facing a national situation where our government leaders are trending toward more socialistic principles. Many government leaders are preaching the sermon that big companies are mean spirited and profit hungry, as though there is another way besides profit for a company to succeed. There seems to be a malaise telling us that individual achievement is bad and entrepreneurism is a spirit that is gone forever. If that is true then America has lost the battle for survival without a shot being fired.

Our current government political philosophy is hopefully temporary. The imbedded American spirit that is inherent to all of us will eventually rise to the surface. I believe we are going through a period where our educational system tends to encourage mediocrity, but that period will eventually end and young people will realize that the "it's all about me" philosophy is a loser in life. Success will once again be a function of individual contribution, creativeness and entrepreneurism. Hard working, creative employees will rise to the top and eventually take that winning spirit back into America's board rooms.

Hopefully our government will again realize that their purpose is not to make life nice for everyone, but to encourage a world that rewards the creators at the expense of those who want to tag along for the ride. To create this environment our American youth must get involved and stay involved in the political process. They must understand the history that made our country great and demand that our country's leaders understand and practice the principles upon which this great nation was founded.

I realize that the readers of this book are not necessarily that young generation and that I am possibly preaching to the choir. We all must do our part to insure that the country's next generation is properly guided by the nation's greatest generation, which includes many who offered their lives to protect the principles of freedom upon which the nation was founded. Let's learn from our mistakes, both corporate and political. If we all do our part we can re-establish our basic principles that hard work will be rewarded with success, corporate and employee loyalty will return, and profit will no longer be a four letter word.

Post-Script

It isn't often that we have the opportunity to look at the facts that face us today and use this information to measure the effectiveness of our past decisions. Too often, as generations develop, they forget the actions and learning of the past and do not apply those lessons learned to future events. To many, the events of the late 1990's have been long forgotten as we struggle to adapt to events that lead us to where we are today. Let me suggest, however, that we pay more attention to our past learning, not to resurface any pain or discomfort, but to apply the learning to prevent making the same mistakes again in the future.

Twenty years after the flurry of mergers and acquisitions of the 1990's, a recent article written by Anthony L. Velocci, Jr., the former Editor-in-chief of Aviation Week & Space Technology, sheds some light on our future expectations in Aerospace and Defense. In his article titled "Transformative

Leadership" published in Aviation Week & Space Technology on March 10, 2014 Velocci recalls the cuts in defense spending from $99 billion in 1990 down to $48 billion in 1996. He recalls the "last supper" that I mentioned earlier in this book which was the event that triggered the downsizing of the Defense industry during the 90's, and what was called the "avalanche" of mergers and acquisitions that followed.

Velocci recognized the group of CEO's that were in charge in the 90's and the fact that they understood that they were facing a fundamentally different market. He gave great praise to those leaders who were forced to do the unpopular thing at the time. He defined the actions of those CEO's as initiating a Darwinian consolidation of the industry that lasted a decade. He points out that we will never know what the industry would have looked like in 2014 if those leaders had failed to correctly assess the harsh market realities and chosen a different course of action. He defined those CEO's as transformative leaders who were just what the country needed at the time. Many of the people who worked in or around the defense industry at the time of this downsizing did not look with the same pride at those industry leaders. But these same critics should look around them today and ask if the same or even more severe actions will soon be upon us.

Velocci reminds us that the size and duration of the congressionally mandated budget cuts will have potentially long term consequences on the defense industry, again. We have always known that the business cycle in the defense industry is variable. Some place the duration of that cycle between 17 and 25 years. Those estimates were, however, derived in times of relative political stability when our nation's leaders recognized the importance of a strong defense in establishing the country's world leadership. During the past decades, military leaders were making military decisions and political decisions were being made by political leaders.

Unfortunately in recent years many of our nation's political leaders seem to be governing with blinders on, not facing the realities of the constant turmoil throughout the world. National priorities seem to have shifted to protecting our social infrastructure rather than protecting our national security and our position of strength throughout the world. Developing strong inspiring leaders and business entrepreneurs has given way to achieving social and income equality with no apparent concern for inventiveness and upward mobility. We seem to have lowered the expectations of our educational system to emphasize fairness and de-emphasize the competitive spirit. With this socialistic trend, is it any wonder that Velocci expresses concern that today's breed of CEO's might not have what it takes to respond to changes that most certainly will take place in the near future?

Velocci is not necessarily predicting another surge in industrial consolidations. but it is not difficult for any learned adult to realize that another period of massive industrial change is coming in the very near future. Velocci states that it is not apparent to him that many of the leaders of today's defense industry have a grand vision for their own company, nor do they have that vision for the greater good of their industry. He also is concerned that today's industry leaders might not be very effective in guiding their companies through the maze of competitive, operational, and political challenges that will define the defense industry for years to come.

It is my opinion and also that of others who have traveled these roads before, that having reduced the defense industrial base to five major defense companies that survive today, there is little room left for further consolidation of these companies. Past experience has shown that the military leaders, if they are consulted, would not likely approve of any further consolidations among the defense prime contractors. Additional consolidation therefore will have to take place at the lower tiers or the prime contractors will get so small that they will be unable to effectively carry out a major weapons development and production program. The future will be very interesting, but it likely will not be very pleasant for the defense industry.

I hope that by presenting the facts and events as they occurred during the early 1990's, I have properly closed the book on the final days of the old Grumman and the current and future of the new Northrop Grumman. Enough time has passed since the acquisition in early 1994 to demonstrate that the efforts and decisions made by Grumman management that turned a friendly merger into an acquisition were indeed the only choices available to the company at that time.

Since the new Northrop Grumman came into existence, many changes have been made to the culture and the geographical makeup of the company. Fortunately the combined heritage of both Northrop and Grumman has been preserved to date. There will certainly continue to be changes that will grow the company to achieve more focus on its core capabilities.

As I have already indicated, the working relationship between the employees and management will, by necessity, continue to change as national priorities and business conditions evolve. I believe that the American working population will continue to realize that creativity and individual achievement are the keys to success and upward mobility in the corporate world. This re-vitalized attitude will cause the successful companies to re-develop their attitude of loyalty toward the work force which in return will create loyalty by the employees toward the company.

Northrop Grumman has already witnessed the ability of its employees to rebound from disappointing setbacks. The terrible months immediately after the acquisition of Grumman caused many good employees to leave the company. But! Many more rebounded and thrived, providing leadership and contributing to the success of their new company. To me, this proves that loyalty and dedication to their company is still very much alive at Northrop Grumman.

I have shown how actions by our government in the past have caused major changes to both Grumman and Northrop. These changes have not always been pleasant but both companies have taken the necessary actions to guarantee their survival. It would be foolhardy to assume that the political process will change quickly, but for the survival of our country it must eventually change. I believe that change will come only if there is enough awareness and outcry by the American public to alter the motives of our politicians. I encourage all Americans, regardless of their political beliefs, to stay aware of the activities of their government and to speak out when our leaders begin to follow a path that strays from the path defined by our country's founders in the Constitution.

America is a great nation because it was made great by its people, their beliefs, and their sacrifices. The foundation of our industrial capability is companies like Northrop and Grumman who provided careers and a fine standard of living for hundreds of thousands of our citizens. With the continued support of its employees and creative leadership by its management, the Northrop Grumman family will continue to demonstrate its greatness for generations to come.

God Bless America

The Grumman E-2 Hawkeye aircraft is an all-weather carrier capable, tactical, airborne, early warning aircraft. This twin turboprop aircraft was designed and developed during the early 1960's and is still in active use today. This aircraft was designed from the ground up to provide for the specific mission of command and control while having complete compatibility with the Navy's Tactical Data System aboard Navy ships. The longevity of this aircraft is testimony to the quality of all Grumman products. The Hawkeye will continue for years to provide the Navy reliable early warning capability. (Photo supplied by the Navy)

31030420R00177

Made in the USA
Middletown, DE
15 April 2016